EMERSON

MUIR

THOREAU

A Photographic Trilogy
of American Wildness

Mount Desert Island, Maine   October 2003

EMERSON

MUIR

THOREAU

A Photographic Trilogy
of American Wildness

SCOT MILLER

LEVENGER PRESS

Published by Levenger Press
420 South Congress Avenue
Delray Beach, Florida 33445 USA
www.levengerpress.com

First Edition 2015

"Nature" by Ralph Waldo Emerson was originally published in 1836 by James Munroe and Company, Boston.

"Walking" by Henry David Thoreau was originally published in *The Atlantic Monthly* magazine in 1862.

"The American Forests" and "The Forests of the Yosemite Park" by John Muir were originally published in *The Atlantic Monthly* magazine in 1897 and 1900, respectively.

Henry David Thoreau's handwritten manuscript leaf from "Walking" that is reproduced on page 187 is from the Thoreau Library of Kevin MacDonnell (The Walden Woods Project Collections at the Thoreau Institute at Walden Woods).

Library of Congress Cataloging-in-Publication Data

Miller, Scot.
  Emerson, Muir, Thoreau : a photographic trilogy of American wildness / Scot Miller.
    pages cm
  Includes index.
  ISBN 978-1-929154-55-5
 1. Forest ecology--United States. 2. Forests and forestry--United States. 3. National parks and reserves--United States.
4. Wilderness areas--United States. 5. American poetry--19th century. I. Emerson, Ralph Waldo, 1803-1882. Nature.
II. Muir, John, 1838-1914. American forests. III. Thoreau, Henry David, 1817-1862. Walking. IV. Title.
  QK938.F6M56 2015
  577.3--dc23
                                        2015005810

Printed on paper from a renewable and sustainable source, using soy-blended inks. Manufactured by Worzalla,
an environmentally responsible printer.

Cover and book design by Danielle Furci
Color veracity by Alfred Guerra
Mim Harrison, Editor

Printed in the USA

CONTENTS

INTRODUCTION

EMERSON, MUIR, THOREAU: BUILDING A BRIDGE

AS an engaged student of the writings of Henry David Thoreau and John Muir, for years it has been apparent to me that Thoreau's writings influenced Muir, but, I often wondered, how much? Thus began a personal journey to build a bridge between these two men who were so important to the early American conservation movement, even though their paths never crossed. In studying their individual influences, one name stood front and center for both: Ralph Waldo Emerson. As the Thoreau scholar Lawrence Buell writes, "The case for Emersonian influence [on Thoreau] is open and shut. World literature offers no more dramatic case of long-term discipleship to a particular 'great' precursor by a young writer later recognized as great in his own right." For his part, John Muir was an avid reader of both Emerson and Thoreau, heavily annotating his personal copies of both men's books, and quoting each in his writings. Pictures of Emerson and Thoreau sat on the mantle in the study of Muir's Martinez, California, home. In the Thoreau-Muir-Emerson circle, it was Emerson who enjoyed personal interactions with both Thoreau and Muir, and included both of them as "one of my men" in a list in his 1871 journal.

This book marries passages from each man's selected work with never-before-published photographs. For Emerson, that work is "Nature" (1836). For Thoreau, it's "Walking" (1862). For Muir, it's "The American Forests" (1897). This is the first book to visually link the philosophies of all three, emphasizing their interconnectedness and the role that their intertwined orbits played in America's environmental coming of age.

Writer, poet, artist, visionary, philosopher, lecturer, transcendentalist, naturalist, botanist, geologist, explorer, adventurer, social reforms advocate, wilderness proponent, conservationist—many of these words can be used to describe each man, and there are numerous ways to approach their writings and philosophies. I come to them from an admittedly distinct point of view: a love and appreciation of nature and a passion for exploring, protecting, and preserving wild spaces. In these respects alone, the combined legacy of Emerson, Muir, and Thoreau is considerable. It is difficult to imagine the modern conservation movement without their influence.

PHILOSOPHER

There is an unbroken circle of ideas in this book that begins and ends with Ralph Waldo Emerson, the Sage of Concord. In his lifetime, Emerson was one of the most widely known and influential authors in America. Both philosophical and naturalistic, his "Nature" essay is credited with laying the foundation of Transcendentalism and defining the ideals of an emerging American conservation and environmental movement. It was groundbreaking, controversial, and thought-provoking. Shortly after "Nature" was published, Thoreau, a senior at Harvard College, checked the book out from the school library not once but twice within a short period of time. After Thoreau graduated from Harvard in 1837, Emerson became his mentor. At Emerson's urging, Thoreau started keeping a daily journal, which he continued with for the rest of his life, and which formed the basis of many of his essays and books. Inspired by Emerson, Thoreau advocated for a more active relationship with nature. He engaged with nature on a daily basis, expanding his thoughts and horizons. He sought out wild places, like Cape Cod and the Maine woods, where he experienced the upsides and downsides of nature. In *The Maine Woods* (1864), he became the first American writer to advocate for preserving lands and creating national preserves.

SAUNTERER

For most of his adult life, Thoreau took daily walks, immersing himself in nature, sharpening his powers of observation, and perfecting the art of sauntering, as he called it. Following Emerson's lead, lecturing became a key source of income. Thoreau considered "Walking" to be one of his most important works, and it was the one lecture that he presented more than any other in the decade before his death. It was so popular, in fact, that he postponed publishing "Walking" for fear of diminishing demand for it on the lecture circuit. It was published shortly after his death.

It is understandable why Thoreau's "Walking" essay became a favorite lecture subject, espousing the joys and benefits of walking, celebrating the wide-open western frontier of America, and arguing for the value of wilderness and man's interaction with it. Along with Emerson's "Nature," "Walking" has become one of the most important essays in America's environmental movement—although, unlike Emerson's works, it wasn't until years after Thoreau's death that people embraced his writings and philosophies. Today his important role in early American nature writing and the emergence of the conservation movement is undeniable.

ACTIVIST

John Muir first became acquainted with the writings of Thoreau and Emerson in the 1860s and was influenced greatly by both. He not only advocated with his writings and lectures but also engaged himself in the political process, becoming a central figure in the debate over land use in our country in the late 1800s and early 1900s. "The American Forests" is a compelling example of how Muir used his writing to interject into an ongoing debate. Published in 1897, the essay was a stinging rebuke to business interests that were pressuring Congress to postpone the enactment of an Executive Order issued by President Grover Cleveland setting aside federal lands for thirteen new national forest reserves in the western states, preserving them from commercial exploitation. Muir's efforts ultimately were successful in helping sway public and congressional opinion.

Emerson and Muir met only one time, in Yosemite, in May 1871. Muir was thirty-three, Emerson nearly sixty-eight. Emerson's relationship with Thoreau, in the end, hadn't turned out totally to his satisfaction; perhaps, after Thoreau's death in 1862, Emerson saw an opportunity for redemption with the young John Muir. Muir was thrilled to engage with Emerson, whom he greatly respected, but was disappointed that Emerson would not camp with him under the stars. The meeting had a profound effect, though, on both men; they continued to correspond, but never again met in person.

The two were from vastly different worlds—Emerson from the old, staid East and Muir from the new, wild West. Emerson thought Muir's talents were being wasted in Yosemite and tried to convince him to move east. Instead, Muir went to the mountains in search of glaciers. He tried to entice Emerson back to Yosemite but was unsuccessful—although he *was* successful in persuading President Theodore Roosevelt to visit Yosemite in 1903 and camp with him, with far-reaching results.

Muir continued to write and publish essays and books. He traveled the world, founded the Sierra Club in 1892, and was instrumental in the formation of the National Park Service in 1916, two years after his death.

THE ONGOING CIRCLE

Thoreau was just forty-four when he died. Emerson lived to seventy-eight and Muir, seventy-six. What might have happened if Thoreau had lived longer? If he had lived another thirty years, he would have seen the creation of our first national parks. What if he and Muir had met? Might Thoreau have advocated and campaigned for, with the support and encouragement of John Muir, wilderness parks in the east, where today they are few and far between?

Better yet, imagine the electricity if all three of these great men had come together. What would have come of it? I like to think that sparks would have flown, each man benefiting from the wisdom and passion of the others.

Free thinkers all, they were not satisfied with the status quo. They expanded boundaries. Emerson conceptualized and illuminated new ideas about relating to nature in both spiritual and physical ways. Inspired by Emerson, Thoreau advocated for an experiential, active relationship with nature, leading by example. At a time when many people saw our natural resources as endless, he recognized the fallacy of this and was the first to write about the need to protect and preserve wild spaces. Influenced greatly by Thoreau and Emerson, Muir took the idea of an experiential and spiritual relationship with nature literally to new heights. Thoreau's Wild became John Muir's Wilderness. Muir became a strong, passionate advocate for wilderness areas and national preserves, and is widely recognized as the father of our national parks.

What would our country look like today without the influences of Emerson, Thoreau, and Muir? Thankfully, this is something we need not imagine because, individually and collectively, they stepped forward, opened eyes, and made good things happen. Emerson, Thoreau, and Muir helped build the bridge to get us here. We are fortunate that we don't have to be wealthy in America to have the opportunity to appreciate wild beauty—we have inherited a wonderful legacy of wild spaces, open to all. It is up to us to carry the legacy forward to future generations.

Scott Miller

Tuolumne River, Yosemite National Park, California   July 17, 2003

Who looks upon a river in a meditative hour,
and is not reminded of the flux of all things?

EMERSON

THE WEST OF WHICH I SPEAK IS BUT ANOTHER NAME FOR THE WILD;

and what I have been preparing to say is, that in Wildness is the preservation of the World.

Life consists with wildness.

The most alive is the wildest. Not yet subdued to man, its presence refreshes him. One who pressed forward incessantly and never rested from his labors, who grew fast and made infinite demands on life, would always find himself in a new country or wilderness, and surrounded by the raw material of life. He would be climbing over the prostrate stems of primitive forest-trees.

THOREAU

All things are moral; and in their boundless changes have an unceasing reference to spiritual nature. Therefore is nature glorious with form, color, and motion...

EMERSON

Yosemite National Park, California   April 23, 2013

Yosemite National Park, California   September 3, 2014

NOTWITHSTANDING ALL THE WASTE AND USE WHICH HAVE BEEN GOING ON UNCHECKED LIKE A STORM FOR MORE THAN TWO CENTURIES, IT IS NOT YET TOO LATE, THOUGH IT IS HIGH TIME, FOR THE GOVERNMENT TO BEGIN A RATIONAL ADMINISTRATION OF ITS FORESTS.

....

In their natural condition, or under wise management, keeping out destructive sheep, preventing fires, selecting the trees that should be cut for lumber, and preserving the young ones and the shrubs and sod of herbaceous vegetation, *these forests would be a never failing fountain of wealth and beauty.*

MUIR

9

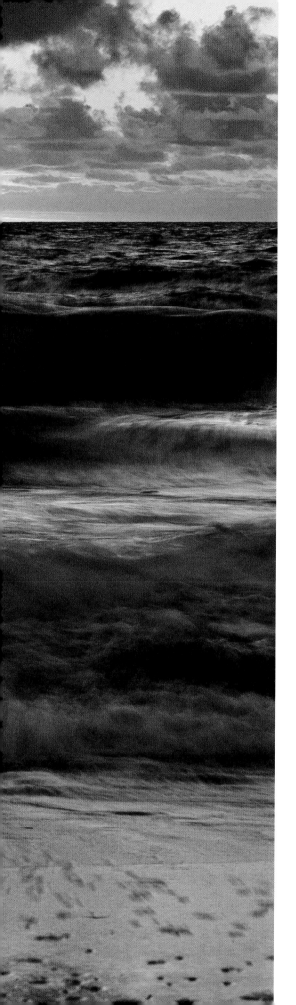

The best moments of life are
these delicious awakenings
of the higher powers, and
the reverential withdrawing
of nature before its God.

EMERSON

Cape Cod National Seashore, Massachusetts   August 24, 2014

...the simple perception of natural forms is a delight. The influence of the forms and actions in nature is so needful to man, that, in its lowest functions, it seems to lie on the confines of commodity and beauty. To the body and mind which have been cramped by noxious work or company, nature is medicinal and restores their tone. The tradesman, the attorney comes out of the din and craft of the street and sees the sky and the woods, and is a man again. In their eternal calm, he finds himself. The health of the eye seems to demand a horizon. *We are never tired, so long as we can see far enough.*

EMERSON

Sierra Nevada Mountains, California   October 2002

Thoreau, when contemplating the destruction of the forests

on the east side of the continent, said that soon the country

would be so bald that every man would have to grow

whiskers to hide its nakedness, but he thanked God that at

least the sky was safe. Had he gone West he would have

found out that the sky was not safe; for all through the

summer months, over most of the mountain regions, the

smoke of mill and forest fires is so thick and black that no

sunbeam can pierce it. THE WHOLE SKY, WITH CLOUDS, SUN, MOON, AND STARS, IS SIMPLY BLOTTED OUT.

MUIR

Bright seas made its border, with wave embroidery and icebergs; gray deserts were outspread in the middle of it, mossy tundras on the north, savannas on the south, and blooming prairies and plains; while lakes and rivers shone through all the vast forests and openings, and happy birds and beasts gave delightful animation.

Everywhere, everywhere over all the blessed continent, there were beauty, and melody, and kindly, wholesome, foodful abundance.

MUIR

Nothing divine dies. All good is eternally reproductive. The beauty of nature reforms itself in the mind, and not for barren contemplation, but for new creation.

ALL MEN ARE IN SOME DEGREE IMPRESSED BY THE FACE OF THE WORLD; SOME MEN EVEN TO DELIGHT. THIS LOVE OF BEAUTY IS TASTE. OTHERS HAVE THE SAME LOVE IN SUCH EXCESS, THAT, NOT CONTENT WITH ADMIRING, THEY SEEK TO EMBODY IT IN NEW FORMS. THE CREATION OF BEAUTY IS ART.

EMERSON

Great Trinity Forest, Dallas, Texas   May 16, 2012

Nature never wears a mean appearance. Neither does the wisest man extort her secret, and lose his curiosity by finding out all her perfection. Nature never became a toy to a wise spirit. The flowers, the animals, the mountains, reflected the wisdom of his best hour, as much as they had delighted the simplicity of his childhood.

EMERSON

Maine Woods   September 30, 2012

We hug the earth—
how rarely we mount!
Methinks we might
elevate ourselves
a little more. We
might climb a tree, at least.
I found my account in
climbing a tree once. It was
a tall white pine, on the
top of a hill; and though
I got well pitched, I was
well paid for it, for I
discovered new mountains
in the horizon which I had
never seen before—so
much more of the earth
and the heavens.

THOREAU

Yosemite National Park, California   September 5, 2014

Where is the literature which gives expression to Nature?

He would be a poet who could impress the winds and streams into his service, to speak for him; who nailed words to their primitive senses, as farmers drive down stakes in the spring, which the frost has heaved; who derived his words as often as he used them—transplanted them to his page with earth adhering to their roots; whose words were so true and fresh and natural that they would appear to expand like the buds at the approach of spring, though they lay half smothered between two musty leaves in a library—aye, to bloom and bear fruit there, after their kind, annually, for the faithful reader, in sympathy with surrounding Nature.

I do not know of any poetry to quote which adequately expresses this yearning for the Wild.

THOREAU

THERE WILL BE A PERIOD OF INDIFFERENCE ON THE PART OF THE RICH, SLEEPY WITH WEALTH, AND OF THE TOILING MILLIONS, SLEEPY WITH POVERTY, most of whom never saw a forest; a period of screaming protest and objection from the plunderers, who are as unconscionable and enterprising as Satan. But light is surely coming, and the friends of destruction will preach and bewail in vain.

MUIR

Yosemite National Park, California   November 1, 2007

This grand tree, *Sequoia sempervirens*, is surpassed in size only by its near relative, *Sequoia gigantea*, or big tree, of the Sierra Nevada, if indeed it is surpassed. The sempervirens is certainly the taller of the two. The gigantea attains a greater girth, and is heavier, more noble in port, and more sublimely beautiful. THESE TWO SEQUOIAS ARE ALL THAT ARE KNOWN TO EXIST IN THE WORLD...

MUIR

"THE HEAVENS OF
AMERICA APPEAR
INFINITELY HIGHER,
THE SKY IS BLUER,
THE AIR IS FRESHER,
the cold is intenser, the moon looks larger,
the stars are brighter, the thunder is
louder, the lightning is vivider, the wind
is stronger, the rain is heavier, the
mountains are higher, the rivers longer,
the forests bigger, the plains broader."

If the moon looks larger here than in
Europe, probably the sun looks larger also.
If the heavens of America appear infinitely
higher, and the stars brighter, *I trust
that these facts are symbolical of
the height to which the philosophy
and poetry and religion of her
inhabitants may one day soar.*

THOREAU

30

Yosemite National Park, California   September 19, 2011

When I behold a rich landscape, it is less to my purpose to recite correctly the order and superposition of the strata, than to know why all thought of multitude is lost in a tranquil sense of unity.

THE LONG SLENDER BARS OF CLOUD FLOAT LIKE FISHES IN THE SEA OF CRIMSON LIGHT. FROM THE EARTH, AS A SHORE, I LOOK OUT INTO THAT SILENT SEA.

EMERSON

Sierra Nevada Mountains, California   September 3, 2014

For I believe that climate does thus react on man—as there is something in the mountain air that feeds the spirit and inspires. Will not man grow to greater perfection intellectually as well as physically under these influences? Or is it unimportant how many foggy days there are in his life? I trust that we shall be more imaginative, that our thoughts will be clearer, fresher, and more ethereal, as our sky—our understanding more comprehensive and broader, like our plains—our intellect generally on a grander scale, like our thunder and lightning, our rivers and mountains and forests—and our hearts shall even correspond in breadth and depth and grandeur to our inland seas.

THOREAU

Buffalo National River, Arkansas   May 17, 2011

EMERSON SAYS THAT THINGS REFUSE TO BE MISMANAGED LONG.

An exception would seem to be found in the case of our forests, which have been mismanaged rather long, and now come desperately near being like smashed eggs and spilt milk. Still, in the long run the world does not move backward.

The making of the far-famed New York Central Park was opposed by even good men, with misguided pluck, perseverance, and ingenuity; but straight right won its way, and now that park is appreciated. So we confidently believe it will be with our great national parks and forest reservations.

MUIR

Eureka Springs, Arkansas   November 1, 2009

When, at rare intervals, some thought visits one, as perchance he is walking on a railroad, then, indeed, the cars go by without his hearing them. But soon, by some inexorable law, our life goes by and the cars return.

THOREAU

Texas Hill Country   March 26, 2007

The shows of day, the dewy morning, the rainbow, mountains, orchards in blossom, stars, moonlight, shadows in still water, and the like, if too eagerly hunted, become shows merely, and mock us with their unreality.

EMERSON

ANY FOOL CAN DESTROY TREES.

THEY CANNOT RUN AWAY; AND IF THEY COULD, THEY WOULD STILL BE DESTROYED,— chased and hunted down as long as fun or a dollar could be got out of their bark hides, branching horns, or magnificent bole backbones. Few that fell trees plant them; nor would planting avail much towards getting back anything like the noble primeval forests. During a man's life only saplings can be grown, in the place of the old trees—tens of centuries old—that have been destroyed. It took more than three thousand years to make some of the trees in these Western woods,—trees that are still standing in perfect strength and beauty, waving and singing in the mighty forests of the Sierra. Through all the wonderful, eventful centuries since Christ's time—and long before that—God has cared for these trees, saved them from drought, disease, avalanches, and a thousand straining, leveling tempests and floods; but he cannot save them from fools,—only Uncle Sam can do that.

MUIR

Nature stretcheth out her arms to embrace man, only let his thoughts be of equal greatness. Willingly does she follow his steps with the rose and the violet, and bend her lines of grandeur and grace to the decoration of her darling child. Only let his thoughts be of equal scope, and the frame will suit the picture.

EMERSON

When I would recreate myself, I seek the darkest wood, the thickest and most interminable and, to the citizen, most dismal, swamp. I enter a swamp as a sacred place, a *sanctum sanctorum*. There is the strength, the marrow, of Nature.

AN ABSOLUTELY NEW PROSPECT IS A GREAT HAPPINESS, AND I CAN STILL GET THIS ANY AFTERNOON. TWO OR THREE HOURS' WALKING WILL CARRY ME TO AS STRANGE A COUNTRY AS I EXPECT EVER TO SEE.

THOREAU

Yosemite National Park, California   June 5, 2011

For nature is not always tricked in holiday attire, but the same scene which yesterday breathed perfume and glittered as for the frolic of the nymphs, is overspread with melancholy to-day. *Nature always wears the colors of the spirit.*

Every spirit builds itself a house, and beyond its house a world, and beyond its world a heaven. Know then that the world exists for you.

EMERSON

I BELIEVE IN THE
FOREST, AND IN
THE MEADOW, AND
IN THE NIGHT IN WHICH
THE CORN GROWS. WE
REQUIRE AN INFUSION OF
HEMLOCK, SPRUCE OR
ARBOR VITAE IN OUR TEA.

*When we walk, we naturally go
to the fields and woods: what
would become of us, if we walked
only in a garden or a mall?*

THOREAU

Yosemite National Park, California   May 1999

White Mountains, New Hampshire   October 1997

For my part, I feel that with regard to Nature I live a sort of border life, on the confines of a world into which I make occasional and transient forays only, and my patriotism and allegiance to the state into whose territories I seem to retreat are those of a moss-trooper.

PERCHANCE THERE WILL APPEAR TO THE TRAVELER SOMETHING, HE KNOWS NOT WHAT, of *laeta* and *glabra*, of joyous and serene, in our very faces. Else to what end does the world go on, and why was America discovered?

THOREAU

The law of harmonic sounds reappears in the harmonic colors. The granite is differenced in its laws only by the more or less of heat from the river that wears it away.

EMERSON

Yosemite National Park, California July 18, 2002

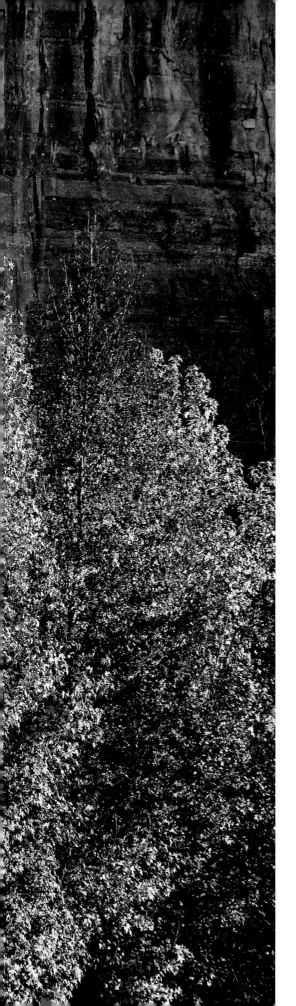

In the woods, we return to reason and faith. There I feel that nothing can befall me in life,—no disgrace, no calamity (leaving me my eyes), which nature cannot repair.

Nature is made to conspire with spirit to emancipate us.

We know more from nature than we can at will communicate. Its light flows into the mind evermore, and we forget its presence.

EMERSON

Indeed the river is a perpetual gala, and boasts each month a new ornament.

The river, as it flows, resembles the air that flows over it; the air resembles the light which traverses it with more subtile currents; the light resembles the heat which rides with it through Space.

EMERSON

Yosemite National Park, California   September 11, 2001

GOLD, GOLD, GOLD! HOW STRONG A VOICE THAT METAL HAS!

Many of the miners find that timber is already becoming scarce and dear on the denuded hills around their mills, and they too are asking for protection of forests, at least against fire. The slow-going, un-thrifty farmers, also, are beginning to realize that when the timber is stripped from the mountains the irrigating streams dry up in summer, and are destructive in winter; that soil, scenery, and everything slips off with the trees: so of course they are coming into the ranks of tree-friends.

That a change from robbery and ruin to a permanent rational policy is urgently needed nobody with the slightest knowledge of American forests will deny.

MUIR

Bodie State Historic Park, California   July 6, 2005

The cool shades of the forest give rise to moist beds and currents of air, and the sod of grasses and the various flowering plants and shrubs thus fostered, together with the network and sponge of tree roots, absorb and hold back the rain and the waters from melting snow, compelling them to ooze and percolate and flow gently through the soil in streams that never dry.

MUIR

Maine Woods   September 25, 2007

These forests were composed of about five hundred species of trees,...lordly monarchs proclaiming the gospel of beauty like apostles.

For many a century after the ice-ploughs were melted, ,nature fed them and dressed them every day; working like a man, a loving, devoted, painstaking gardener; fingering every leaf and flower and mossy furrowed bole; bending, trimming, modeling, balancing, painting them with the loveliest colors; bringing over them now clouds with cooling shadows and showers, now sunshine; fanning them with gentle winds and rustling their leaves; exercising them in every fibre with storms, and pruning them; loading them with flowers and fruit, loading them with snow, and ever making them more beautiful as the years rolled by.

MUIR

Yosemite National Park, California   July 17, 2002

My spirits infallibly rise in proportion to the outward dreariness. Give me the ocean, the desert, or the wilderness!

THOREAU

"Nature has not only outlined her works on a larger scale, but has painted the whole picture with brighter, and more costly colors than she used in delineating and in beautifying the Old World...."

HERE IS THIS VAST, SAVAGE, HOVERING MOTHER OF OURS, NATURE, lying all around, with such beauty, and such affection for her children, as the leopard; and yet we are so early weaned from her breast to society...

THOREAU

Walden Pond State Reservation, Massachusetts
October 23, 2008

Lyndon B. Johnson National Historical Park, Texas   May 27, 2010

In short, all good things are wild and free. There is something in a strain of music, whether produced by an instrument or by the human voice—take the sound of a bugle in a summer night, for instance—which by its wildness, to speak without satire, reminds me of the cries emitted by wild beasts in their native forests. It is so much of their wildness as I can understand. Give me for my friends and neighbors wild men, not tame ones.

I LOVE EVEN TO SEE THE DOMESTIC ANIMALS REASSERT THEIR NATIVE RIGHTS—any evidence that they have not wholly lost their original wild habits and vigor; as when my neighbor's cow breaks out of her pasture early in the spring and boldly swims the river, a cold, gray tide, twenty-five or thirty rods wide, swollen by the melted snow. It is the buffalo crossing the Mississippi.

THOREAU

Yosemite National Park, California   April 18, 2005

We have heard of a Society for the Diffusion of Useful Knowledge. It is said that knowledge is power, and the like. Methinks there is equal need of a Society for the Diffusion of Useful Ignorance, what we will call Beautiful Knowledge, a knowledge useful in a higher sense: *for what is most of our boasted so-called knowledge but a conceit that we know something, which robs us of the advantage of our actual ignorance?*

I WOULD SAY TO THE SOCIETY FOR THE DIFFUSION OF USEFUL KNOWLEDGE, SOMETIMES, GO TO GRASS. YOU HAVE EATEN HAY LONG ENOUGH. THE SPRING HAS COME WITH ITS GREEN CROP.

THOREAU

My desire for knowledge is intermittent, but my desire to bathe my head in atmospheres unknown to my feet is perennial and constant. The highest that we can attain to is not Knowledge, but Sympathy with Intelligence.

THOREAU

Yosemite National Park, California   September 16, 2011

I AM THE LOVER OF UNCONTAINED AND IMMORTAL BEAUTY.

In the wilderness, I find something more dear and connate than in streets or villages. In the tranquil landscape, and especially in the distant line of the horizon, man beholds somewhat as beautiful as his own nature.

I have no hostility to nature, but a child's love to it.

EMERSON

Buffalo National River, Arkansas   September 28, 2008

A nobler want of man is served by nature, namely, the love of Beauty.

THE ANCIENT GREEKS CALLED THE WORLD κόσμος, BEAUTY.

EMERSON

*...the dawn of a new day
in forestry is breaking....
Merely what belongs to all
alike is reserved...*

MUIR

Yosemite National Park, California   July 17, 2010

Falmouth, Maine   July 30, 2014

A single object is only so far beautiful as it suggests this universal grace. The poet, the painter, the sculptor, the musician, the architect, seek each to concentrate this radiance of the world on one point, and each in his several work to satisfy the love of beauty which stimulates him to produce.

THE EYE IS THE BEST OF ARTISTS.

EMERSON

The beauty that shimmers in the yellow afternoons of October, who ever could clutch it? Go forth to find it, and it is gone: 't is only a mirage as you look from the windows of diligence.

. . . .

There is still another aspect under which the beauty of the world may be viewed, namely, as it becomes an object of the intellect. BESIDE THE RELATION OF THINGS TO VIRTUE, THEY HAVE A RELATION TO THOUGHT.

EMERSON

Pennsylvania Dutch Country   July 1998

I SUPPOSE WE NEED NOT GO MOURNING THE BUFFALOES. IN THE NATURE OF THINGS THEY HAD TO GIVE PLACE TO BETTER CATTLE, THOUGH THE CHANGE MIGHT HAVE BEEN MADE WITHOUT BARBAROUS WICKEDNESS. LIKEWISE MANY OF NATURE'S FIVE HUNDRED KINDS OF WILD TREES HAD TO MAKE WAY FOR ORCHARDS AND CORNFIELDS.

MUIR

The moral influence of nature upon every individual is that amount of truth which it illustrates to him. Who can estimate this? Who can guess how much firmness the sea-beaten rock has taught the fisherman?

EMERSON

Gloucester, Massachusetts   October 2004

AMERICAN FORESTS! THE GLORY OF THE WORLD!

Surveyed thus from the east to the west, from the north to the south, they are rich beyond thought, immortal, immeasurable...

With such variety, harmony, and triumphant exuberance, even nature, it would seem, might have rested content with the forests of North America, and planted no more.

MUIR

It is hard for me to believe that I shall find fair landscapes or sufficient wildness and freedom behind the eastern horizon. I am not excited by the prospect of a walk thither; but I believe that the forest which I see in the western horizon stretches uninterruptedly toward the setting sun, and there are no towns nor cities in it of enough consequence to disturb me. Let me live where I will, on this side is the city, on that the wilderness, and ever I am leaving the city more and more, and withdrawing into the wilderness. I should not lay so much stress on this fact, if I did not believe that something like this is the prevailing tendency of my countrymen. I MUST WALK TOWARD OREGON, AND NOT TOWARD EUROPE.

. . . .

We go eastward to realize history and study the works of art and literature, retracing the steps of the race; *we go westward as into the future, with a spirit of enterprise and adventure.*

THOREAU

Yosemite National Park, California   September 8, 2008

Caddo Lake, City of Uncertain, Texas   October 30, 2012

Hope and the future for me are not in lawns and cultivated fields, not in towns and cities, but in the impervious and quaking swamps. When, formerly, I have analyzed my partiality for some farm which I had contemplated purchasing, I have frequently found that I was attracted solely by a few square rods of impermeable and unfathomable bog—a natural sink in one corner of it. That was the jewel which dazzled me. *I derive more of my subsistence from the swamps which surround my native town than from the cultivated gardens in the village.*

THOREAU

The heavens change every moment,
and reflect their glory or gloom on
the plains beneath.

EMERSON

Yosemite National Park, California   July 22, 2009

I am alarmed when it happens that
I have walked a mile into the woods
bodily, without getting there in spirit.

IN MY WALKS I WOULD FAIN
RETURN TO MY SENSES.
WHAT BUSINESS HAVE I IN THE
WOODS, IF I AM THINKING OF
SOMETHING OUT OF THE WOODS?

THOREAU

Buffalo National River, Arkansas   October 31, 2008

TIMBER IS AS NECESSARY
AS BREAD, AND NO SCHEME
OF MANAGEMENT FAILING TO
RECOGNIZE AND PROPERLY
PROVIDE FOR THIS WANT CAN
POSSIBLY BE MAINTAINED.

MUIR

Maine Woods   June 22, 2011

EVERY OTHER CIVILIZED NATION IN THE WORLD HAS BEEN COMPELLED TO CARE FOR ITS FORESTS, AND SO MUST WE...

Now it is plain that the forests are not inexhaustible, and that quick measures must be taken if ruin is to be avoided. Year by year the remnant is growing smaller before the axe and fire, while the laws in existence provide neither for the protection of the timber from destruction nor for its use where it is most needed.

MUIR

The forests of America, however slighted by man, must have been a great delight to God; for they were the best he ever planted. The whole continent was a garden, and from the beginning it seemed to be favored above all the other wild parks and gardens of the globe. To prepare the ground, it was rolled and sifted in seas with infinite loving deliberation and fore-thought, lifted into the light, submerged and warmed over and over again, pressed and crumpled into folds and ridges, mountains, and hills, subsoiled with heaving volcanic fires, ploughed and ground and sculptured into scenery and soil with glaciers and rivers,—every feature growing and changing from beauty to beauty, higher and higher. And in the fullness of time it was planted in groves, and belts, and broad, exuberant, mantling forests, with the largest, most varied, most fruitful, and most beautiful trees in the world.

MUIR

To the northward, over Maine
and Ottawa, rose hosts of spiry,
rosiny evergreens,—white pine
and spruce, hemlock and cedar,
shoulder to shoulder, laden with purple cones, their
myriad needles sparkling and shimmering,
covering hills and swamps, rocky headlands and
domes, ever bravely aspiring and seeking the sky;
the ground in their shade now snow-clad and
frozen, now mossy and flowery; beaver meadows
here and there, full of lilies and grass; lakes
gleaming like eyes, and a silvery embroidery of
rivers and creeks watering and brightening
all the vast glad wilderness.

MUIR

Baxter State Park, Maine   September 28, 2012

A truly good book is something as natural, and as unexpectedly and unaccountably fair and perfect, as a wild-flower discovered on the prairies of the West or in the jungles of the East. Genius is a light which makes the darkness visible, like the lightning's flash, which perchance shatters the temple of knowledge itself—and not a taper lighted at the hearthstone of the race, which pales before the light of common day.

THOREAU

BUT NOT ONE DENUDED ACRE IN A HUNDRED IS ALLOWED TO RAISE A NEW FOREST GROWTH. ON THE CONTRARY, ALL THE BRAINS, RELIGION, AND SUPERSTITION OF THE NEIGHBORHOOD ARE BROUGHT INTO PLAY TO PREVENT A NEW GROWTH.

The sprouts from the roots and stumps are cut off again and again, with zealous concern as to the best time and method of making death sure. In the clearings of one of the largest mills on the coast we found thirty men at work, last summer, cutting off redwood shoots "in the dark of the moon," claiming that all the stumps and roots cleared at this auspicious time would send up no more shoots. Anyhow, these vigorous, almost immortal trees are killed at last, and black stumps are now their only monuments over most of the chopped and burned areas.

MUIR

Chamberlain Lake, Maine   June 26, 2010

To the southward stretched dark,
level-topped cypresses in knobby,
tangled swamps, grassy savannas
in the midst of them like lakes
of light, groves of gay, sparkling
spice-trees, magnolias and palms,
glossy-leaved and blooming and
shining continually.

MUIR

Caddo Lake, City of Uncertain, Texas   May 19, 2014

The inhabitants of cities suppose that the country landscape is pleasant only half the year. I please myself with the graces of the winter scenery, and believe that we are as much touched by it as by the genial influences of summer.

EMERSON

Stonewall, Texas   January 17, 2007

Yosemite National Park, California   April 21, 2010

THE WONDERFUL ADVANCE MADE IN THE LAST FEW YEARS, IN CREATING FOUR NATIONAL PARKS IN THE WEST, AND THIRTY FOREST RESERVATIONS, EMBRACING NEARLY FORTY MILLION ACRES; and in the planting of the borders of streets and highways and spacious parks in all the great cities, to satisfy the natural taste and hunger for landscape beauty and righteousness that God has put, in some measure, into every human being and animal, shows the trend of awakening public opinion.

MUIR

Concord, Massachusetts   November 2, 2011

*And as the eye is the best composer,
so light is the first of painters.*

....

*Nature is a sea of forms radically
alike and even unique.* A leaf, a sun-beam,
a landscape, the ocean, make an analogous impression on
the mind. What is common to them all,—that perfectness
and harmony, is beauty.

EMERSON

San Juan National Forest, Colorado   September 30, 2014

THENCE STILL WESTWARD
SWEPT THE FORESTS TO RIGHT AND
LEFT AROUND GRASSY PLAINS AND
DESERTS A THOUSAND MILES WIDE:
irrepressible hosts of spruce and pine, aspen and willow, nut-pine and juniper, cactus and yucca, caring nothing for drought, extending undaunted from mountain to mountain, over mesa and desert, to join the darkening multitudes of pines that covered the high Rocky ranges and the glorious forests along the coast of the moist and balmy Pacific...

Here the forests reached their highest development. Hence they went wavering northward over icy Alaska, brave spruce and fir, poplar and birch, by the coasts and the rivers, to within sight of the Arctic Ocean.

MUIR

HE WHO SITS STILL IN A HOUSE ALL THE TIME MAY BE THE GREATEST VAGRANT OF ALL; but the saunterer, in the good sense, is no more vagrant than the meandering river, which is all the while sedulously seeking the shortest course to the sea.

I think that I cannot preserve my health and spirits, unless I spend four hours a day at least—and it is commonly more than that—sauntering through the woods and over the hills and fields, absolutely free from all worldly engagements.

THOREAU

What is it that makes it so hard sometimes to determine whither we will walk? *I believe that there is a subtle magnetism in Nature,* which, if we unconsciously yield to it, will direct us aright. It is not indifferent to us which way we walk.

· ·

When I go out of the house for a walk, uncertain as yet whither I will bend my steps, and submit myself to my instinct to decide for me, I find, strange and whimsical as it may seem, THAT I FINALLY AND INEVITABLY SETTLE SOUTHWEST, TOWARD SOME PARTICULAR WOOD OR MEADOW OR DESERTED PASTURE OR HILL IN THAT DIRECTION.

THOREAU

Lyndon B. Johnson National Historical Park, Texas   August 10, 2014

I, who cannot stay in my chamber for a single day without acquiring some rust, and when sometimes I have stolen forth for a walk at the eleventh hour, or four o'clock in the afternoon, too late to redeem the day, when the shades of night were already beginning to be mingled with the daylight, have felt as if I had committed some sin to be atoned for—I confess that I am astonished at the power of endurance, to say nothing of the moral insensibility, of my neighbors who confine themselves to shops and offices the whole day for weeks and months, aye, and years almost together.

Moreover, you must walk like a camel, which is said to be the only beast which ruminates when walking. When a traveler asked Wordsworth's servant to show him her master's study, she answered, "HERE IS HIS LIBRARY, BUT HIS STUDY IS OUT OF DOORS."

THOREAU

'The active enchantment'

RALPH WALDO EMERSON

NATURE
1836

A subtle change of countless rings
The next unto the farthest brings;
The eye reads omens where it goes,
And speaks all languages the rose;
And, striving to be man, the worm
Mounts through all the spires of form.

INTRODUCTION

OUR age is retrospective. It builds the sepulchres of the fathers. It writes biographies, histories, and criticism. The foregoing generations beheld God and nature face to face; we, through their eyes. Why should not we also enjoy an original relation to the universe? Why should not we have a poetry and philosophy of insight and not of tradition, and a religion by revelation to us, and not the history of theirs? Embosomed for a season in nature, whose floods of life stream around and through us, and invite us by the powers they supply, to action proportioned to nature, why should we grope among the dry bones of the past, or put the living generation into masquerade out of its faded wardrobe? The sun shines to-day also. There is more wool and flax in the fields. There are new lands, new men, new thoughts. Let us demand our own works and laws and worship.

Undoubtedly we have no questions to ask which are unanswerable. We must trust the perfection of the creation so far as to believe that whatever curiosity the order of things has awakened in our minds, the order of things can satisfy. Every man's condition is a solution in hieroglyphic to those inquiries he would put. He acts it as life, before he apprehends it as truth. In like manner, nature is already, in its forms and tendencies, describing its own design. Let us interrogate the great apparition that shines so peacefully around us. Let us inquire, to what end is nature?

All science has one aim, namely, to find a theory of nature. We have theories of races and of functions, but scarcely yet a remote approach to an idea of creation. We are now so far from the road to truth, that religious teachers dispute and hate each other, and speculative men are esteemed unsound and frivolous. But to a sound judgment, the most abstract truth is the most practical. Whenever a true theory appears, it will be its own evidence. Its test is, that it will explain all phenomena. Now many are thought not only unexplained but inexplicable; as language, sleep, madness, dreams, beasts, sex.

Philosophically considered, the universe is composed of Nature and the Soul. Strictly speaking, therefore, all that is separate from us, all which Philosophy distinguishes as the NOT ME, that is, both nature and art, all other men and my own body, must be ranked under this name, NATURE. In enumerating the values of nature and casting up their sum,

I shall use the word in both senses;—in its common and in its philosophical import. In inquiries so general as our present one, the inaccuracy is not material; no confusion of thought will occur. *Nature*, in the common sense, refers to essences unchanged by man; space, the air, the river, the leaf. *Art* is applied to the mixture of his will with the same things, as in a house, a canal, a statue, a picture. But his operations taken together are so insignificant, a little chipping, baking, patching, and washing, that in an impression so grand as that of the world on the human mind, they do not vary the result.

NATURE

TO go into solitude, a man needs to retire as much from his chamber as from society. I am not solitary whilst I read and write, though nobody is with me. But if a man would be alone, let him look at the stars. The rays that come from those heavenly worlds will separate between him and what he touches. One might think the atmosphere was made transparent with this design, to give man, in the heavenly bodies, the perpetual presence of the sublime. Seen in the streets of cities, how great they are! If the stars should appear one night in a thousand years, how would men believe and adore; and preserve for many generations the remembrance of the city of God which had been shown! But every night come out these envoys of beauty, and light the universe with their admonishing smile.

The stars awaken a certain reverence, because though always present, they are inaccessible; but all natural objects make a kindred impression, when the mind is open to their influence. Nature never wears a mean appearance. Neither does the wisest man extort her secret, and lose his curiosity by finding out all her perfection. Nature never became a toy to a wise spirit. The flowers, the animals, the mountains, reflected the wisdom of his best hour, as much as they had delighted the simplicity of his childhood.

When we speak of nature in this manner, we have a distinct but most poetical sense in the mind. We mean the integrity of impression made by manifold natural objects. It is this which distinguishes the stick of timber of the wood-cutter from the tree of the poet. The charming landscape which I saw this morning is indubitably made up of some twenty or thirty farms. Miller owns this field, Locke that, and Manning the woodland beyond. But none of them owns the landscape. There is a property in the horizon which no man has but he whose eye can integrate all the parts, that is, the poet. This is the best part of these men's farms, yet to this their warranty-deeds give no title.

To speak truly, few adult persons can see nature. Most persons do not see the sun. At least they have a very superficial seeing. The sun illuminates only the eye of the man, but shines into the eye and the heart of the child. The lover of nature is he whose inward and outward senses are still truly adjusted to each other; who has retained the spirit of infancy even into the era of manhood. His intercourse with heaven and earth becomes part of his daily food. In the presence of nature a wild delight runs through the man, in spite of real sorrows. Nature says,—he is my creature, and maugre all his impertinent griefs, he shall be glad with me. Not the sun or the summer alone, but every hour and season yields its tribute of delight; for every hour and change corresponds to and authorizes a different state of the mind, from breathless noon to grimmest midnight. Nature is a setting that fits equally well a comic or a mourning piece. In good health, the air is a cordial of incredible virtue. Crossing a bare common, in snow puddles, at twilight, under a clouded sky, without having in my thoughts any occurrence of special good fortune, I have enjoyed a perfect exhilaration. I am glad to the brink of fear. In the woods, too, a man casts off his years, as the snake his slough, and at what period soever of life is always a child. In the woods is perpetual youth. Within these plantations of God, a decorum and sanctity reign, a perennial festival is dressed, and the guest sees not how he should tire of them in a thousand years. In the woods, we return to reason and faith. There I feel that nothing can befall me in life,—no disgrace, no calamity (leaving me my eyes), which nature cannot repair. Standing on the bare ground,—my head bathed by the blithe air and uplifted into infinite space,—all mean egotism vanishes. I become a transparent eyeball; I am nothing; I see all; the currents of the Universal Being circulate through me; I am part or particle of God. The name of the nearest friend sounds then foreign and accidental: to be brothers, to be acquaintances, master or servant, is then a trifle and a disturbance. I am the lover of uncontained and immortal beauty. In the wilderness, I find something more dear and connate than in streets or villages. In the tranquil landscape, and especially in the distant line of the horizon, man beholds somewhat as beautiful as his own nature.

The greatest delight which the fields and woods minister is the suggestion of an occult relation between man and the vegetable. I am not alone and unacknowledged. They nod to me, and I to them. The waving of the boughs in the storm is new to me and old. It takes me by surprise, and yet is not unknown. Its effect is like that of a higher thought or a better emotion coming over me, when I deemed I was thinking justly or doing right.

Yet it is certain that the power to produce this delight does not reside in nature, but in man, or in a harmony of both. It is necessary to use these pleasures with great temperance. For nature is not always tricked in holiday attire, but the same scene which yesterday breathed perfume and glittered as for the frolic of the nymphs, is overspread with melancholy to-day. Nature always wears the colors of the spirit. To a man laboring under calamity, the heat of his own fire hath sadness in it. Then there is a kind of contempt of the landscape felt by him who has just lost by death a dear friend. The sky is less grand as it shuts down over less worth in the population.

II COMMODITY

WHOEVER considers the final cause of the world will discern a multitude of uses that enter as parts into that result. They all admit of being thrown into one of the following classes; Commodity; Beauty; Language; and Disciplinec

Under the general name of commodity, I rank all those advantages which our senses owe to nature. This, of course, is a benefit which is temporary and mediate, not ultimate, like its service to the soul. Yet although low, it is perfect in its kind, and is the only use of nature which all men apprehend. The misery of man appears like childish petulance, when we explore the steady and prodigal provision that has been made for his support and delight on this green ball which floats him through the heavens. What angels invented these splendid ornaments, these rich conveniences, this ocean of air above, this ocean of water beneath, this firmament of earth between? this zodiac of lights, this tent of dropping clouds, this striped coat of climates, this fourfold year? Beasts, fire, water, stones, and corn serve him. The field is at once his floor, his work-yard, his play-ground, his garden, and his bed.

> **"More servants wait on man**
> **Than he'll take notice of."**

Nature, in its ministry to man, is not only the material, but is also the process and the result. All the parts incessantly work into each other's hands for the profit of man. The wind sows the seed; the sun evaporates the sea; the wind blows the vapor to the field; the ice, on the other side of the planet, condenses rain on this; the rain feeds the plant; the plant feeds the animal; and thus the endless circulations of the divine charity nourish man.

The useful arts are reproductions or new combinations by the wit of man, of the same natural benefactors. He no longer waits for favoring gales, but by means of steam, he realizes the fable of Aeolus's bag, and carries the two and thirty winds in the boiler of his boat. To diminish friction, he paves the road with iron bars, and, mounting a coach with a ship-load of men, animals, and merchandise behind him, he darts through the country, from town to town, like an eagle or a swallow through the air. By the aggregate of these aids, how is the face of the world changed, from the era of Noah to that of Napoleon! The private poor man hath cities, ships, canals, bridges, built for him. He goes to the post-office, and the human race run on his errands; to the book-shop, and the human race read and write of all that happens, for him; to the court-house, and nations repair his wrongs. He sets his house upon the road, and the human race go forth every morning, and shovel out the snow, and cut a path for him.

But there is no need of specifying particulars in this class of uses. The catalogue is endless, and the examples so obvious, that I shall leave them to the reader's reflection, with the general remark, that this mercenary benefit is one which has respect to a farther good. A man is fed, not that he may be fed, but that he may work.

 BEAUTY

A NOBLER want of man is served by nature, namely, the love of Beauty.

The ancient Greeks called the world κόσμος, beauty. Such is the constitution of all things, or such the plastic power of the human eye, that the primary forms, as the sky, the mountain, the tree, the animal, give us a delight *in and for themselves*; a pleasure arising from outline, color, motion, and grouping. This seems partly owing to the eye itself. The eye is the best of artists. By the mutual action of its structure and of the laws of light, perspective is produced, which integrates every mass of objects, of what character soever, into a well colored and shaded globe, so that where the particular objects are mean and unaffecting, the landscape which they compose is round and symmetrical. And as the eye is the best composer, so light is the first of painters. There is no object so foul that intense light will not make beautiful. And the stimulus it affords to the sense, and a sort of infinitude which it hath, like space and time, make all matter gay. Even the corpse has its own beauty. But besides this general grace diffused over nature, almost all the individual forms are agreeable to the eye, as is proved by our endless imitations of some of them, as the acorn, the grape, the pine-cone, the wheat-ear, the egg, the wings and forms of most birds, the lion's claw, the serpent, the butterfly, sea-shells, flames, clouds, buds, leaves, and the forms of many trees, as the palm.

For better consideration, we may distribute the aspects of Beauty in a threefold manner.

1. First, the simple perception of natural forms is a delight. The influence of the forms and actions in nature is so needful to man, that, in its lowest functions, it seems to lie on the confines of commodity and beauty. To the body and mind which have been cramped by noxious work or company, nature is medicinal and restores their tone. The tradesman, the attorney comes out of the din and craft of the street and sees the sky and the woods, and is a man again. In their eternal calm, he finds himself. The health of the eye seems to demand a horizon. We are never tired, so long as we can see far enough.

But in other hours, Nature satisfies by its loveliness, and without any mixture of corporeal benefit. I see the spectacle of morning from the hilltop over against my house, from daybreak to sunrise, with emotions which an angel might share. The long slender bars of cloud float like fishes in the sea of crimson light. From the earth, as a shore, I look out into that silent sea. I seem to partake its rapid transformations: the active enchantment reaches my dust, and I dilate and conspire with the morning wind. How does Nature deify us with a few and cheap elements! Give me health and a day, and I will make the pomp of emperors ridiculous. The dawn is my Assyria; the sunset and moonrise my Paphos, and unimaginable realms of faerie; broad noon shall be my England of the senses and the understanding; the night shall be my Germany of mystic philosophy and dreams.

Not less excellent, except for our less susceptibility in the afternoon, was the charm, last evening, of a January sunset. The western clouds divided and subdivided themselves into pink flakes modulated with tints of unspeakable softness, and the air had so much life and sweetness that it was a pain to come within doors. What was it that nature would say? Was there no meaning in the live repose of the valley behind the mill, and which Homer or Shakspeare could not re-form for me in words? The leafless trees become spires of flame in the sunset, with the blue east for their background, and the stars of the dead calices of flowers, and every withered stem and stubble rimed with frost, contribute something to the mute music.

The inhabitants of cities suppose that the country landscape is pleasant only half the year. I please myself with the graces of the winter scenery, and believe that we are as much touched by it as by the genial influences of summer. To the attentive eye, each moment of the year has its own beauty, and in the same field, it beholds, every hour, a picture which was never seen before, and which shall never be seen again. The heavens change every moment, and reflect their glory or gloom on the plains beneath. The state of the crop in the surrounding farms alters the expression of the earth from week to week. The succession of native plants in the pastures and roadsides, which makes the silent clock by which time tells the summer hours, will make even the divisions of the day sensible to a keen observer. The tribes of birds and insects, like the plants punctual to their time, follow each other, and the year has room for all. By water-courses, the variety is greater. In July, the blue pontederia or pickerel-weed blooms in large beds in the shallow parts of our pleasant river, and swarms with yellow butterflies in continual motion. Art cannot rival this pomp of purple and gold. Indeed the river is a perpetual gala, and boasts each month a new ornament.

But this beauty of Nature which is seen and felt as beauty, is the least part. The shows of day, the dewy morning, the rainbow, mountains, orchards in blossom, stars, moonlight, shadows in still water, and the like, if too eagerly hunted, become shows merely, and mock us with their unreality. Go out of the house to see the moon, and 't is mere tinsel; it will not please as when its light shines upon your necessary journey. The beauty that shimmers in the yellow afternoons of October, who ever could clutch it? Go forth to find it, and it is gone: 't is only a mirage as you look from the windows of diligence.

2. The presence of a higher, namely, of the spiritual element is essential to its perfection. The high and divine beauty which can be loved without effeminacy, is that which is found in combination with the human will. Beauty is the mark God sets upon virtue. Every natural action is graceful. Every heroic act is also decent, and causes the place and the bystanders to shine. We are taught by great actions that the universe is the property of every individual in it. Every rational creature has all nature for his dowry and estate. It is his, if he will. He may divest himself of it; he may creep into a corner, and abdicate his kingdom, as most men do, but he is entitled to the world by his constitution. In

proportion to the energy of his thought and will, he takes up the world into himself. "All those things for which men plough, build, or sail, obey virtue;" said Sallust. "The winds and waves," said Gibbon, "are always on the side of the ablest navigators." So are the sun and moon and all the stars of heaven. When a noble act is done,—perchance in a scene of great natural beauty; when Leonidas and his three hundred martyrs consume one day in dying, and the sun and moon come each and look at them once in the steep defile of Thermopylae; when Arnold Winkelried, in the high Alps, under the shadow of the avalanche, gathers in his side a sheaf of Austrian spears to break the line for his comrades; are not these heroes entitled to add the beauty of the scene to the beauty of the deed? When the bark of Columbus nears the shore of America;—before it, the beach lined with savages, fleeing out of all their huts of cane; the sea behind; and the purple mountains of the Indian Archipelago around, can we separate the man from the living picture? Does not the New World clothe his form with her palm-groves and savannahs as fit drapery? Ever does natural beauty steal in like air, and envelope great actions. When Sir Harry Vane was dragged up the Tower-hill, sitting on a sled, to suffer death, as the champion of the English laws, one of the multitude cried out to him, "You never sate on so glorious a seat!" Charles II., to intimidate the citizens of London, caused the patriot Lord Russell to be drawn in an open coach through the principal streets of the city on his way to the scaffold. "But," his biographer says, "the multitude imagined they saw liberty and virtue sitting by his side." In private places, among sordid objects, an act of truth or heroism seems at once to draw to itself the sky as its temple, the sun as its candle. Nature stretcheth out her arms to embrace man, only let his thoughts be of equal greatness. Willingly does she follow his steps with the rose and the violet, and bend her lines of grandeur and grace to the decoration of her darling child. Only let his thoughts be of equal scope, and the frame will suit the picture. A virtuous man is in unison with her works, and makes the central figure of the visible sphere. Homer, Pindar, Socrates, Phocion, associate themselves fitly in our memory with the geography and climate of Greece. The visible heavens and earth sympathize with Jesus. And in common life, whosoever has seen a person of powerful character and happy genius, will have remarked how easily he took all things along with him,—the persons, the opinions, and the day, and nature became ancillary to a man.

3. There is still another aspect under which the beauty of the world may be viewed, namely, as it becomes an object of the intellect. Beside the relation of things to virtue, they have a relation to thought. The intellect searches out the absolute order of things as they stand in the mind of God, and without the colors of affection. The intellectual and the active powers seem to succeed each other, and the exclusive activity of the one generates the exclusive activity of the other. There is something unfriendly in each to the other, but they are like the alternate periods of feeding and working in animals; each prepares and will be followed by the other. Therefore does beauty, which, in relation to actions, as we have seen, comes unsought, and comes because it is unsought, remain for the apprehension and pursuit of the intellect; and then again, in its turn, of the active power. Nothing divine dies. All good is eternally reproductive. The beauty of nature reforms itself in the mind, and not for barren contemplation, but for new creation.

All men are in some degree impressed by the face of the world; some men even to delight. This love of beauty is Taste. Others have the same love in such excess, that, not content with admiring, they seek to embody it in new forms. The creation of beauty is Art.

The production of a work of art throws a light upon the mystery of humanity. A work of art is an abstract or epitome of the world. It is the result or expression of nature, in miniature. For although the works of nature are innumerable and all different, the result or the expression of them all is similar and single. Nature is a sea of forms radically alike and even unique. A leaf, a sun-beam, a landscape, the ocean, make an analogous impression on the mind. What is common to them all,—that perfectness and harmony, is beauty. The standard of beauty is the entire circuit of natural forms,—the totality of nature; which the Italians expressed by defining beauty "il più nell' uno." Nothing is quite beautiful alone: nothing but is beautiful in the whole. A single object is only so far beautiful as it suggests this universal grace. The poet, the painter, the sculptor, the musician, the architect, seek each to concentrate this radiance of the world on one point, and each in his several work to satisfy the love of beauty which stimulates him to produce. Thus is Art a nature passed through the alembic of man. Thus in art, does Nature work through the will of a man filled with the beauty of her first works.

The world thus exists to the soul to satisfy the desire of beauty. This element I call an ultimate end. No reason can be asked or given why the soul seeks beauty. Beauty, in its largest and profoundest sense, is one expression for the universe. God is the all-fair. Truth, and goodness, and beauty, are but different faces of the same All. But beauty in nature is not ultimate. It is the herald of inward and eternal beauty, and is not alone a solid and satisfactory good. It must stand as a part, and not as yet the last or highest expression of the final cause of Nature.

 LANGUAGE

LANGUAGE is a third use which Nature subserves to man. Nature is the vehicle of thought, and in a simple, double, and threefold degree.

> 1. **Words are signs of natural facts.**
> 2. **Particular natural facts are symbols of particular spiritual facts.**
> 3. **Nature is the symbol of spirit.**

1. Words are signs of natural facts. The use of natural history is to give us aid in supernatural history: the use of the outer creation, to give us language for the beings and changes of the inward creation. Every word which is used to express a moral or intellectual fact, if traced to its root, is found to be borrowed from some material appearance. *Right* means *straight*; *wrong* means *twisted*. *Spirit* primarily means *wind*; *transgression*, the crossing of a *line*; *supercilious*, the *raising of the eyebrow*. We say the *heart* to express emotion, the *head* to denote thought; and *thought* and *emotion* are words borrowed from sensible things, and now appropriated to spiritual nature. Most of the process by which this transformation is made, is hidden from us in the remote time when language was framed; but the same tendency may be daily observed in children. Children and savages use only nouns or names of things, which they convert into verbs, and apply to analogous mental acts.

2. But this origin of all words that convey a spiritual import,—so conspicuous a fact in the history of language,—is our least debt to nature. It is not words only that are emblematic; it is things which are emblematic. Every natural fact is a symbol of some spiritual fact. Every appearance in nature corresponds to some state of the mind, and that state of the mind can only be described by presenting that natural appearance as its picture. An enraged man is a lion, a cunning man is a fox, a firm man is a rock, a learned man is a torch. A lamb is innocence; a snake is subtle spite; flowers express to us the delicate affections. Light and darkness are our familiar expression for knowledge and ignorance; and heat for love. Visible distance behind and before us, is respectively our image of memory and hope.

Who looks upon a river in a meditative hour, and is not reminded of the flux of all things? Throw a stone into the stream, and the circles that propagate themselves are the beautiful type of all influence. Man is conscious of a universal soul within or behind his individual life, wherein, as in a firmament, the natures of Justice, Truth, Love, Freedom, arise and shine. This universal soul, he calls Reason: it is not mine, or thine, or his, but we are its; we are its property and men. And the blue sky in which the private earth is buried, the sky with its eternal calm, and full of everlasting orbs, is the type of Reason. That which intellectually considered we call Reason, considered in relation to nature, we call Spirit. Spirit is the Creator. Spirit hath life in itself. And man in all ages and countries embodies it in his language as the FATHER.

It is easily seen that there is nothing lucky or capricious in these analogies, but that they are constant, and pervade nature. These are not the dreams of a few poets, here and there, but man is an analogist, and studies relations in all objects. He is placed in the centre of beings, and a ray of relation passes from every other being to him. And neither can man be understood without these objects, nor these objects without man. All the facts in natural history taken by themselves, have no value, but are barren, like a single sex. But marry it to human history, and it is full of life. Whole floras, all Linnaeus' and Buffon's volumes, are dry catalogues of facts; but the most trivial of these facts, the habit of a plant, the organs, or work, or noise of an insect, applied to the illustration of a fact in intellectual philosophy, or in any way associated to human nature, affects us in the most lively and agreeable manner. The seed of a plant,—to what affecting analogies in the nature of man is that little fruit made use of, in all discourse, up to the voice of Paul, who calls the human corpse a seed,—"It is sown a natural body; it is raised a spiritual body." The motion of the earth round its axis, and round the sun, makes the day and the year. These are certain amounts of brute light and heat. But is there no intent of an analogy between man's life and the seasons? And do the seasons gain no grandeur or pathos from that analogy? The instincts of the ant are very unimportant, considered as the ant's; but the moment a ray of relation is seen to extend from it to man, and the little drudge is seen to be a monitor, a little body with a mighty heart, then all its habits, even that said to be recently observed, that it never sleeps, become sublime.

Because of this radical correspondence between visible things and human thoughts, savages, who have only what is necessary, converse in figures. As we go back in history, language becomes more picturesque, until its infancy, when it is all poetry; or all spiritual facts are represented by natural symbols. The same symbols are found to make the original elements of all languages. It has moreover been observed, that the idioms of all languages approach each other in passages of the greatest eloquence and power. And as this is the first language, so is it the last. This immediate dependence of language upon nature, this conversion of an outward phenomenon into a type of somewhat in human life, never loses its power to affect us. It is this which gives that piquancy to the conversation of a strong-natured farmer or back-woodsman, which all men relish.

A man's power to connect his thought with its proper symbol, and so to utter it, depends on the simplicity of his character, that is, upon his love of truth and his desire to communicate it without loss. The corruption of man is followed by the corruption of language. When simplicity of character and the sovereignty of ideas is broken up by the prevalence of secondary desires,—the desire of riches, of pleasure, of power, and of praise,—and duplicity and falsehood take place of simplicity and truth, the power over nature as an interpreter of the will is in a degree lost; new imagery ceases to be created, and old words are perverted to stand for things which are not; a paper currency is employed, when there is no bullion in the vaults. In due time the fraud is manifest, and words lose all power to stimulate the understanding or the affections. Hundreds of writers may be found in every long-civilized nation who for a short time believe and make others believe that they see and utter truths, who do not of themselves clothe one thought in its natural garment, but who feed unconsciously on the language created by the primary writers of the country, those, namely, who hold primarily on nature.

But wise men pierce this rotten diction and fasten words again to visible things; so that picturesque language is at once a commanding certificate that he who employs it is a man in alliance with truth and God. The moment our discourse rises above the ground line of familiar facts and is inflamed with passion or exalted by thought, it clothes itself in images. A man conversing in earnest, if he watch his intellectual processes, will find that a material image more or less luminous arises in his mind, cotemporaneous with every thought, which furnishes the vestment of the thought. Hence, good writing and brilliant discourse are perpetual allegories. This imagery is spontaneous. It is the blending of experience with the present action of the mind. It is proper creation. It is the working of the Original Cause through the instruments he has already made.

These facts may suggest the advantage which the country-life possesses, for a powerful mind, over the artificial and curtailed life of cities. We know more from nature than we can at will communicate. Its light flows into the mind evermore, and we forget its presence. The poet, the orator, bred in the woods, whose senses have been nourished by their fair and appeasing changes, year after year, without design and without heed,—shall not lose their lesson altogether, in the roar of cities or the broil of politics. Long hereafter, amidst agitation and terror in national councils,—in the hour of revolution,—these solemn images shall reappear in their morning lustre, as fit symbols and words of the thoughts which the passing events shall awaken. At the call of a noble sentiment, again the woods wave, the pines murmur, the river rolls and shines, and the cattle low upon the mountains, as he saw and heard them in his infancy. And with these forms, the spells of persuasion, the keys of power are put into his hands.

3. We are thus assisted by natural objects in the expression of particular meanings. But how great a language to convey such pepper-corn informations! Did it need such noble races of creatures, this profusion of forms, this host of orbs in heaven, to furnish man with the dictionary and grammar of his municipal speech? Whilst we use this grand cipher to expedite the affairs of our pot and kettle, we feel that we have not yet put it to its use, neither are able. We are like travellers using the cinders of a volcano to roast their eggs. Whilst we see that it always stands ready to clothe what we would say, we cannot avoid the question whether the characters are not significant of themselves. Have mountains, and waves, and skies, no significance but what we consciously give them when we employ them as emblems of our thoughts? The world is emblematic. Parts of speech are metaphors, because the whole of nature is a metaphor of the human mind. The laws of moral nature answer to those of matter as face to face in a glass. "The visible world and the relation of its parts, is the dial plate of the invisible." The axioms of physics translate the laws of ethics. Thus, "the whole is greater than its part;" "reaction is equal to action;" "the smallest weight may be made to lift the greatest, the difference of weight being compensated by time;" and many the like propositions, which have an ethical as well as physical sense. These propositions have a much more extensive and universal sense when applied to human life, than when confined to technical use.

In like manner, the memorable words of history and the proverbs of nations consist usually of a natural fact, selected as a picture or parable of a moral truth. Thus; A rolling stone gathers no moss; A bird in the hand is worth two in the bush; A cripple in the right way will beat a racer in the wrong; Make hay while the sun shines; 'T is hard to carry a full cup even; Vinegar is the son of wine; The last ounce broke the camel's back; Long-lived trees make roots first;—and the like. In their primary sense these are trivial facts, but we repeat them for the value of their analogical import. What is true of proverbs, is true of all fables, parables, and allegories.

This relation between the mind and matter is not fancied by some poet, but stands in the will of God, and so is free to be known by all men. It appears to men, or it does not appear. When in fortunate hours we ponder this miracle, the wise man doubts if at all other times he is not blind and deaf;

—"Can such things be,
And overcome us like a summer's cloud,
Without our special wonder?"

for the universe becomes transparent, and the light of higher laws than its own shines through it. It is the standing problem which has exercised the wonder and the study of every fine genius since the world began; from the era of the Egyptians and the Brahmins to that of Pythagoras, of Plato, of Bacon, of Leibnitz, of Swedenborg. There sits the Sphinx at the road-side, and from age to age, as each prophet comes by, he tries his fortune at reading her riddle. There seems to be a necessity in spirit to manifest itself in material forms; and day and night, river and storm, beast and bird, acid and alkali, preëxist in necessary Ideas in the mind of God, and are what they are by virtue of preceding affections in the world of spirit. A Fact is the end or last issue of spirit. The visible creation is the terminus or the circumference of the invisible world. "Material objects," said a French philosopher, "are necessarily kinds of *scoriae* of the substantial thoughts of the Creator, which must always preserve an exact relation to their first origin; in other words, visible nature must have a spiritual and moral side."

This doctrine is abstruse, and though the images of "garment," "scoriae," "mirror," etc., may stimulate the fancy, we must summon the aid of subtler and more vital expositors to make it plain. "Every scripture is to be interpreted by the same spirit which gave it forth,"—is the fundamental law of criticism. A life in harmony with Nature, the love of truth and of virtue, will purge the eyes to understand her text. By degrees we may come to know the primitive sense of the permanent objects of nature, so that the world shall be to us an open book, and every form significant of its hidden life and final cause.

A new interest surprises us, whilst, under the view now suggested, we contemplate the fearful extent and multitude of objects; since "every object rightly seen, unlocks a new faculty of the soul." That which was unconscious truth, becomes, when interpreted and defined in an object, a part of the domain of knowledge,—a new weapon in the magazine of power.

 DISCIPLINE

IN view of the significance of nature, we arrive at once at a new fact, that nature is a discipline. This use of the world includes the preceding uses, as parts of itself.

Space, time, society, labor, climate, food, locomotion, the animals, the mechanical forces, give us sincerest lessons, day by day, whose meaning is unlimited. They educate both the Understanding and the Reason. Every property of matter is a school for the understanding,—its solidity or resistance, its inertia, its extension, its figure, its divisibility. The understanding adds, divides, combines, measures, and finds nutriment and room for its activity in this worthy scene. Meantime, Reason transfers all these lessons into its own world of thought, by perceiving the analogy that marries Matter and Mind.

1. Nature is a discipline of the understanding in intellectual truths. Our dealing with sensible objects is a constant

exercise in the necessary lessons of difference, of likeness, of order, of being and seeming, of progressive arrangement; of ascent from particular to general; of combination to one end of manifold forces. Proportioned to the importance of the organ to be formed, is the extreme care with which its tuition is provided,—a care pretermitted in no single case. What tedious training, day after day, year after year, never ending, to form the common sense; what continual reproduction of annoyances, inconveniences, dilemmas; what rejoicing over us of little men; what disputing of prices, what reckonings of interest,—and all to form the Hand of the mind;—to instruct us that "good thoughts are no better than good dreams, unless they be executed!"

The same good office is performed by Property and its filial systems of debt and credit. Debt, grinding debt, whose iron face the widow, the orphan, and the sons of genius fear and hate;—debt, which consumes so much time, which so cripples and disheartens a great spirit with cares that seem so base, is a preceptor whose lessons cannot be forgone, and is needed most by those who suffer from it most. Moreover, property, which has been well compared to snow,—"if it fall level to-day, it will be blown into drifts to-morrow,"—is the surface action of internal machinery, like the index on the face of a clock. Whilst now it is the gymnastics of the understanding, it is hiving, in the foresight of the spirit, experience in profounder laws.

The whole character and fortune of the individual are affected by the least inequalities in the culture of the understanding; for example, in the perception of differences. Therefore is Space, and therefore Time, that man may know that things are not huddled and lumped, but sundered and individual. A bell and a plough have each their use, and neither can do the office of the other. Water is good to drink, coal to burn, wool to wear; but wool cannot be drunk, nor water spun, nor coal eaten. The wise man shows his wisdom in separation, in gradation, and his scale of creatures and of merits is as wide as nature. The foolish have no range in their scale, but suppose every man is as every other man. What is not good they call the worst, and what is not hateful, they call the best.

In like manner, what good heed Nature forms in us! She pardons no mistakes. Her yea is yea, and her nay, nay.

The first steps in Agriculture, Astronomy, Zoölogy (those first steps which the farmer, the hunter, and the sailor take), teach that Nature's dice are always loaded; that in her heaps and rubbish are concealed sure and useful results.

How calmly and genially the mind apprehends one after another the laws of physics! What noble emotions dilate the mortal as he enters into the counsels of the creation, and feels by knowledge the privilege to BE! His insight refines him. The beauty of nature shines in his own breast. Man is greater that he can see this, and the universe less, because Time and Space relations vanish as laws are known.

Here again we are impressed and even daunted by the immense Universe to be explored. "What we know, is a point to what we do not know." Open any recent journal of science, and weigh the problems suggested concerning Light, Heat, Electricity, Magnetism, Physiology, Geology, and judge whether the interest of natural science is likely to be soon exhausted.

Passing by many particulars of the discipline of nature, we must not omit to specify two.

The exercise of the Will or the lesson of power, is taught in every event. From the child's successive possession of his several senses up to the hour when he saith, "Thy will be done!" he is learning the secret that he can reduce under his will not only particular events but great classes, nay, the whole series of events, and so conform all facts to his character. Nature is thoroughly mediate. It is made to serve. It receives the dominion of man as meekly as the ass on which the Saviour rode. It offers all its kingdoms to man as the raw material which he may mould into what is useful. Man is never weary of working it up. He forges the subtile and delicate air into wise and melodious words, and gives them wing as angels of persuasion and command. One after another his victorious thought comes up with and reduces all things, until the world becomes, at last, only a realized will,—the double of the man.

2. Sensible objects conform to the premonitions of Reason and reflect the conscience. All things are moral; and in their boundless changes have an unceasing reference to spiritual nature. Therefore is nature glorious with form, color, and motion; that every globe in the remotest heaven, every chemical change from the rudest crystal up to the laws of life, every change of vegetation from the first principle of growth in the eye of a leaf, to the tropical forest and antediluvian coal-mine, every animal function from the sponge up to Hercules, shall hint or thunder to man the laws of right and wrong, and echo the Ten Commandments. Therefore is Nature ever the ally of Religion: lends all her pomp and riches to the religious sentiment. Prophet and priest, David, Isaiah, Jesus, have drawn deeply from this source. This ethical character so penetrates the bone and marrow of nature, as to seem the end for which it was made. Whatever private purpose is answered by any member or part, this is its public and universal function, and is never omitted. Nothing in nature is exhausted in its first use. When a thing has served an end to the uttermost, it is wholly new for an ulterior service. In God, every end is converted into a new means. Thus the use of commodity, regarded by itself, is mean and squalid. But it is to the mind an education in the doctrine of Use, namely, that a thing is good only so far as it serves; that a conspiring of parts and efforts to the production of an end is essential to any being. The first and gross manifestation of this truth is our inevitable and hated training in values and wants, in corn and meat.

It has already been illustrated, that every natural process is a version of a moral sentence. The moral law lies at the centre of nature and radiates to the circumference. It is the pith and marrow of every substance, every relation, and every process. All things with which we deal, preach to us. What is a farm but a mute gospel? The chaff and the wheat, weeds and plants, blight, rain, insects, sun,—it is a sacred emblem from the first furrow of spring to the last stack which the snow of winter overtakes in the fields. But the sailor, the shepherd, the miner, the merchant, in their several resorts, have each an experience precisely parallel, and leading to the same conclusion: because all organizations are radically alike. Nor can it be doubted that this moral sentiment which thus scents the air, grows in the grain, and impregnates the waters of the world, is caught by man and sinks into his soul. The moral influence of nature upon every individual is that amount of truth which it illustrates to him. Who can estimate this? Who can guess how much firmness the sea-beaten rock has taught the fisherman? how much tranquillity has been reflected to man from the azure sky, over whose unspotted deeps the winds forevermore drive flocks of stormy clouds, and leave no wrinkle or stain? how much industry and providence and affection we have caught from the pantomime of brutes? What a searching preacher of self-command is the varying phenomenon of Health!

Herein is especially apprehended the unity of Nature,—the unity in variety,—which meets us everywhere. All the endless variety of things make an identical impression. Xenophanes complained in his old age, that, look where he would, all things hastened back to Unity. He was weary of seeing the same entity in the tedious variety of forms. The fable of Proteus has a cordial truth. A leaf, a drop, a crystal, a moment of time is related to the whole, and partakes of the perfection of the whole. Each particle is a microcosm, and faithfully renders the likeness of the world.

Not only resemblances exist in things whose analogy is obvious, as when we detect the type of the human hand in the flipper of the fossil saurus, but also in objects wherein there is great superficial unlikeness. Thus architecture is called "frozen music," by De Staël and Goethe. Vitruvius thought an architect should be a musician. "A Gothic church," said Coleridge, "is a petrified religion." Michael Angelo maintained, that, to an architect, a knowledge of anatomy is essential. In Haydn's oratorios, the notes present to the imagination not only motions, as of the snake, the stag, and the elephant, but colors also; as the green grass. The law of harmonic sounds reappears in the harmonic colors. The granite is differenced in its laws only by the more or less of heat from the river that wears it away. The river, as it flows, resembles the air that flows over it; the air resembles the light which traverses it with more subtile currents; the light resembles the heat which rides with it through Space. Each creature is only a modification of the other; the likeness in them is more than the difference, and their radical law is one and the same. A rule of one art, or a law of one organization, holds true throughout nature. So intimate is this Unity, that, it is easily seen, it lies under the undermost garment of Nature, and betrays its source in Universal Spirit. For it pervades Thought also. Every universal truth which we express in words, implies or supposes every other truth. *Omne verum vero consonat.* It is like a great circle on a sphere, comprising all possible circles; which, however, may be drawn and comprise it in like manner. Every such truth is the absolute Ens seen from one side. But it has innumerable sides.

The central Unity is still more conspicuous in actions. Words are finite organs of the infinite mind. They cannot cover the dimensions of what is in truth. They break, chop, and impoverish it. An action is the perfection and publication of thought. A right action seems to fill the eye, and to be related to all nature. "The wise man, in doing one thing, does all; or, in the one thing he does rightly, he sees the likeness of all which is done rightly."

Words and actions are not the attributes of brute nature. They introduce us to the human form, of which all other organizations appear to be degradations. When this appears among so many that surround it, the spirit prefers it to all others. It says, "From such as this have I drawn joy and knowledge; in such as this have I found and beheld myself; I will speak to it; it can speak again; it can yield me thought already formed and alive." In fact, the eye,—the mind,—is always accompanied by these forms, male and female; and these are incomparably the richest informations of the power and order that lie at the heart of things. Unfortunately every one of them bears the marks as of some injury; is marred and superficially defective. Nevertheless, far different from all deaf and dumb nature around them, these all rest like fountain-pipes on the unfathomed sea of thought, and virtue whereto they alone, of all organizations, are the entrances.

It were a pleasant inquiry to follow into detail their ministry to our education, but where would it stop? We are associated in adolescent and adult life with some friends, who, like skies and waters, are coextensive with our idea; who, answering each to a certain affection of the soul, satisfy our desire on that side; whom we lack power to put at such focal distance from us, that we can mend or even analyze them. We cannot choose but love them. When much intercourse with a friend has supplied us with a standard of excellence, and has increased our respect for the resources of God who thus sends a real person to outgo our ideal; when he has, moreover, become an object of thought, and, whilst his character retains all its unconscious effect, is converted in the mind into solid and sweet wisdom,—it is a sign to us that his office is closing, and he is commonly withdrawn from our sight in a short time.

 IDEALISM

THUS is the unspeakable but intelligible and practicable meaning of the world conveyed to man, the immortal pupil, in every object of sense. To this one end of Discipline, all parts of nature conspire.

A noble doubt perpetually suggests itself,—whether this end be not the Final Cause of the Universe; and whether nature outwardly exists. It is a sufficient account of that Appearance we call the World, that God will teach a human mind, and so makes it the receiver of a certain number of congruent sensations, which we call sun and moon, man and woman, house and trade. In my utter impotence to test the authenticity of the report of my senses, to know whether the impressions they make on me correspond with outlying objects, what difference does it make, whether Orion is up there in heaven, or some god paints the image in the firmament of the soul? The relations of parts and the end of the whole remaining the same, what is the difference, whether land and sea interact, and worlds revolve and intermingle without number or end,—deep yawning under deep, and galaxy balancing galaxy, throughout absolute space,—or whether, without relations of time and space, the same appearances are inscribed in the constant faith of man? Whether nature enjoy a substantial existence without, or is only in the apocalypse of the mind, it is alike useful and alike venerable to me. Be it what it may, it is ideal to me so long as I cannot try the accuracy of my senses.

The frivolous make themselves merry with the Ideal theory, as if its consequences were burlesque; as if it affected the stability of nature. It surely does not. God never jests with us, and will not compromise the end of nature, by permitting any inconsequence in its procession. Any distrust of the permanence of laws would paralyze the faculties of man. Their permanence is sacredly respected, and his faith therein is perfect. The wheels and springs of man are all set to the hypothesis of the permanence of nature. We are not built like a ship to be tossed, but like a house to stand. It is a natural consequence of this structure, that so long as the active powers predominate over the reflective, we resist with indignation any hint that nature is more short-lived or mutable than spirit. The broker, the wheelwright, the carpenter, the tollman, are much displeased at the intimation.

But whilst we acquiesce entirely in the permanence of natural laws, the question of the absolute existence of nature still remains open. It is the uniform effect of culture on the human mind, not to shake our faith in the stability of particular phenomena, as of heat, water, azote; but to lead us to regard nature as a phenomenon, not a substance; to attribute necessary existence to spirit; to esteem nature as an accident and an effect.

To the senses and the unrenewed understanding, belongs a sort of instinctive belief in the absolute existence of nature. In their view, man and nature are indissolubly joined. Things are ultimates, and they never look beyond their sphere. The presence of Reason mars this faith. The first effort of thought tends to relax this despotism of the senses, which binds us to nature as if we were a part of it, and shows us nature aloof, and, as it were, afloat. Until this higher agency intervened, the animal eye sees, with wonderful accuracy, sharp outlines and colored surfaces. When the eye of Reason opens, to outline and surface are at once added grace and expression. These proceed from imagination and affection, and abate somewhat of the angular distinctness of objects. If the Reason be stimulated to more earnest vision, outlines and surfaces become transparent, and are no longer seen; causes and spirits are seen through them. The best moments of life are these delicious awakenings of the higher powers, and the reverential withdrawing of nature before its God.

Let us proceed to indicate the effects of culture.

1. Our first institution in the Ideal philosophy is a hint from Nature herself.

Nature is made to conspire with spirit to emancipate us. Certain mechanical changes, a small alteration in our local position, apprizes us of a dualism. We are strangely affected by seeing the shore from a moving ship, from a balloon, or through the tints of an unusual sky. The least change in our point of view gives the whole world a pictorial air. A man who seldom rides, needs only to get into a coach and traverse his own town, to turn the street into a puppet-show. The men, the women,—talking, running, bartering, fighting,—the earnest mechanic, the lounger, the beggar, the boys, the dogs, are unrealized at once, or, at least, wholly detached from all relation to the observer, and seen as apparent, not substantial beings. What new thoughts are suggested by seeing a face of country quite familiar, in the rapid movement of the railroad car! Nay, the most wonted objects, (make a very slight change in the point of vision,) please us most. In a camera obscura, the butcher's cart, and the figure of one of our own family amuse us. So a portrait of a well-known face gratifies us. Turn the eyes upside down, by looking at the landscape through your legs, and how agreeable is the picture, though you have seen it any time these twenty years!

In these cases, by mechanical means, is suggested the difference between the observer and the spectacle—between man and nature. Hence arises a pleasure mixed with awe; I may say, a low degree of the sublime is felt from the fact, probably, that man is hereby apprized, that, whilst the world is a spectacle, something in himself is stable.

2. In a higher manner the poet communicates the same pleasure. By a few strokes he delineates, as on air, the sun, the mountain, the camp, the city, the hero, the maiden, not different from what we know them, but only lifted from the ground and afloat before the eye. He unfixes the land and the sea, makes them revolve around the axis of his primary thought, and disposes them anew. Possessed himself by a heroic passion, he uses matter as symbols of it. The sensual man conforms thoughts to things; the poet conforms things to his thoughts. The one esteems nature as rooted and fast; the other, as fluid, and impresses his being thereon. To him, the refractory world is ductile and flexible; he invests dust and stones with humanity, and makes them the words of the Reason. The Imagination may be defined to be the use which the Reason makes of the material world. Shakspeare possesses the power of subordinating nature for the purposes of expression, beyond all poets. His imperial muse tosses the creation like a bauble from hand to hand, and uses it to embody any caprice of thought that is uppermost in his mind. The remotest spaces of nature are visited, and the farthest sundered things are brought together, by a subtile spiritual connection. We are made aware that magnitude of material things is relative, and all objects shrink and expand to serve the passion of the poet. Thus in his sonnets, the lays of birds, the scents and dyes of flowers he finds to be the *shadow* of his beloved; time, which keeps her from him, is his *chest*; the suspicion she has awakened, is her *ornament*;

> The ornament of beauty is Suspect,
> A crow which flies in heaven's sweetest air.

His passion is not the fruit of chance; it swells, as he speaks, to a city, or a state.

> No, it was builded far from accident;
> It suffers not in smiling pomp, nor falls
> Under the brow of thralling discontent;
> It fears not policy, that heretic,
> That works on leases of short numbered hours,
> But all alone stands hugely politic.

In the strength of his constancy, the Pyramids seem to him recent and transitory. The freshness of youth and love dazzles him with its resemblance to morning;

> Take those lips away
> Which so sweetly were forsworn;

> And those eyes,—the break of day,
> Lights that do mislead the morn.

The wild beauty of this hyperbole, I may say in passing, it would not be easy to match in literature.

This transfiguration which all material objects undergo through the passion of the poet,—this power which he exerts to dwarf the great, to magnify the small,—might be illustrated by a thousand examples from his Plays. I have before me the Tempest, and will cite only these few lines.

> ARIEL. The strong based promontory
> Have I made shake, and by the spurs plucked up
> The pine and cedar.

Prospero calls for music to soothe the frantic Alonzo, and his companions;

> A solemn air, and the best comforter
> To an unsettled fancy, cure thy brains
> Now useless, boiled within thy skull.

Again;

> The charm dissolves apace,
> And, as the morning steals upon the night,
> Melting the darkness, so their rising senses
> Begin to chase the ignorant fumes that mantle
> Their clearer reason.
> Their understanding
> Begins to swell: and the approaching tide
> Will shortly fill the reasonable shores
> That now lie foul and muddy.

The perception of real affinities between events (that is to say, of *ideal* affinities, for those only are real), enables the poet thus to make free with the most imposing forms and phenomena of the world, and to assert the predominance of the soul.

3. Whilst thus the poet animates nature with his own thoughts, he differs from the philosopher only herein, that the one proposes Beauty as his main end; the other Truth. But the philosopher, not less than the poet, postpones the apparent order and relations of things to the empire of thought. "The problem of philosophy," according to Plato, "is, for all that exists conditionally, to find a ground unconditioned and absolute." It proceeds on the faith that a law determines all phenomena, which being known, the phenomena can be predicted. That law, when in the mind, is an idea. Its beauty is infinite. The true philosopher and the true poet are one, and a beauty, which is truth, and a truth, which is beauty, is the aim of both. Is not the charm of one of Plato's or Aristotle's definitions strictly like that of the Antigone of Sophocles? It is, in both cases, that a spiritual life has been imparted to nature; that the solid seeming block of matter has been pervaded and dissolved by a thought; that this feeble human being has penetrated the vast masses of nature with an informing soul, and recognised itself in their harmony, that is, seized their law. In physics,

when this is attained, the memory disburthens itself of its cumbrous catalogues of particulars, and carries centuries of observation in a single formula.

Thus even in physics, the material is degraded before the spiritual. The astronomer, the geometer, rely on their irrefragable analysis, and disdain the results of observation. The sublime remark of Euler on his law of arches, "This will be found contrary to all experience, yet is true;" had already transferred nature into the mind, and left matter like an outcast corpse.

4. Intellectual science has been observed to beget invariably a doubt of the existence of matter. Turgot said, "He that has never doubted the existence of matter, may be assured he has no aptitude for metaphysical inquiries." It fastens the attention upon immortal necessary uncreated natures, that is, upon Ideas; and in their presence we feel that the outward circumstance is a dream and a shade. Whilst we wait in this Olympus of gods, we think of nature as an appendix to the soul. We ascend into their region, and know that these are the thoughts of the Supreme Being. "These are they who were set up from everlasting, from the beginning, or ever the earth was. When he prepared the heavens, they were there; when he established the clouds above, when he strengthened the fountains of the deep. Then they were by him, as one brought up with him. Of them took he counsel."

Their influence is proportionate. As objects of science they are accessible to few men. Yet all men are capable of being raised by piety or by passion, into their region. And no man touches these divine natures, without becoming, in some degree, himself divine. Like a new soul, they renew the body. We become physically nimble and lightsome; we tread on air; life is no longer irksome, and we think it will never be so. No man fears age or misfortune or death in their serene company, for he is transported out of the district of change. Whilst we behold unveiled the nature of Justice and Truth, we learn the difference between the absolute and the conditional or relative. We apprehend the absolute. As it were, for the first time, *we exist*. We become immortal, for we learn that time and space are relations of matter; that with a perception of truth or a virtuous will they have no affinity.

5. Finally, religion and ethics, which may be fitly called the practice of ideas, or the introduction of ideas into life, have an analogous effect with all lower culture, in degrading nature and suggesting its dependence on spirit. Ethics and religion differ herein; that the one is the system of human duties commencing from man; the other, from God. Religion includes the personality of God; Ethics does not. They are one to our present design. They both put nature under foot. The first and last lesson of religion is, "The things that are seen, are temporal; the things that are unseen, are eternal." It puts an affront upon nature. It does that for the unschooled, which philosophy does for Berkeley and Viasa. The uniform language that may be heard in the churches of the most ignorant sects is—"Contemn the unsubstantial shows of the world; they are vanities, dreams, shadows, unrealities; seek the realities of religion." The devotee flouts nature. Some theosophists have arrived at a certain hostility and indignation towards matter, as the Manichean and Plotinus. They distrusted in themselves any looking back to these flesh-pots of Egypt. Plotinus was ashamed of his body. In short, they might all say of matter, what Michael Angelo said of external beauty, "It is the frail and weary weed, in which God dresses the soul which he has called into time."

It appears that motion, poetry, physical and intellectual science, and religion, all tend to affect our convictions of the reality of the external world. But I own there is something ungrateful in expanding too curiously the particulars of the general proposition, that all culture tends to imbue us with idealism. I have no hostility to nature, but a child's love to it. I expand and live in the warm day like corn and melons. Let us speak her fair. I do not wish to fling stones at my beautiful mother, nor soil my gentle nest. I only wish to indicate the true position of nature in regard to man, wherein to establish man all right education tends; as the ground which to attain is the object of human life, that is, of man's connection with nature. Culture inverts the vulgar views of nature, and brings the mind to call that apparent which it uses to call real, and that real which it uses to call visionary. Children, it is true, believe in the external world. The belief that it appears only, is an afterthought, but with culture this faith will as surely arise on the mind as did the first.

The advantage of the ideal theory over the popular faith is this, that it presents the world in precisely that view which is most desirable to the mind. It is, in fact, the view which Reason, both speculative and practical, that is, philosophy and virtue, take. For seen in the light of thought, the world always is phenomenal; and virtue subordinates it to the mind. Idealism sees the world in God. It beholds the whole circle of persons and things, of actions and events, of country and religion, not as painfully accumulated, atom after atom, act after act, in an aged creeping Past, but as one vast picture which God paints on the instant eternity for the contemplation of the soul. Therefore the soul holds itself off from a too trivial and microscopic study of the universal tablet. It respects the end too much to immerse itself in the means. It sees something more important in Christianity than the scandals of ecclesiastical history or the niceties of criticism; and, very incurious concerning persons or miracles, and not at all disturbed by chasms of historical evidence, it accepts from God the phenomenon, as it finds it, as the pure and awful form of religion in the world. It is not hot and passionate at the appearance of what it calls its own good or bad fortune, at the union or opposition of other persons. No man is its enemy. It accepts whatsoever befalls, as part of its lesson. It is a watcher more than a doer, and it is a doer, only that it may the better watch.

VII SPIRIT

IT is essential to a true theory of nature and of man, that it should contain somewhat progressive. Uses that are exhausted or that may be, and facts that end in the statement, cannot be all that is true of this brave lodging wherein man is harbored, and wherein all his faculties find appropriate and endless exercise. And all the uses of nature admit of being summed in one, which yields the activity of man an infinite scope. Through all its kingdoms, to the suburbs and outskirts of things, it is faithful to the cause whence it had its origin. It always speaks of Spirit. It suggests the absolute. It is a perpetual effect. It is a great shadow pointing always to the sun behind us.

The aspect of Nature is devout. Like the figure of Jesus, she stands with bended head, and hands folded upon the breast. The happiest man is he who learns from nature the lesson of worship.

Of that ineffable essence which we call Spirit, he that thinks most, will say least. We can foresee God in the coarse, and, as it were, distant phenomena of matter; but when we try to define and describe himself, both language and thought desert us, and we are as helpless as fools and savages. That essence refuses to be recorded in propositions, but when man has worshipped him intellectually, the noblest ministry of nature is to stand as the apparition of God. It is the organ through which the universal spirit speaks to the individual, and strives to lead back the individual to it.

When we consider Spirit, we see that the views already presented do not include the whole circumference of man. We must add some related thoughts.

Three problems are put by nature to the mind; What is matter? Whence is it? and Whereto? The first of these questions only, the ideal theory answers. Idealism saith: matter is a phenomenon, not a substance. Idealism acquaints us with the total disparity between the evidence of our own being and the evidence of the world's being. The one is perfect; the other, incapable of any assurance; the mind is a part of the nature of things; the world is a divine dream, from which we may presently awake to the glories and certainties of day. Idealism is a hypothesis to account for nature by other principles than those of carpentry and chemistry. Yet, if it only deny the existence of matter, it does not satisfy the demands of the spirit. It leaves God out of me. It leaves me in the splendid labyrinth of my perceptions, to wander without end. Then the heart resists it, because it balks the affections in denying substantive being to men and women. Nature is so pervaded with human life that there is something of humanity in all and in every particular. But this theory makes nature foreign to me, and does not account for that consanguinity which we acknowledge to it.

Let it stand, then, in the present state of our knowledge, merely as a useful introductory hypothesis, serving to apprize us of the eternal distinction between the soul and the world.

But when, following the invisible steps of thought, we come to inquire, Whence is matter? and Whereto? many truths arise to us out of the recesses of consciousness. We learn that the highest is present to the soul of man; that the dread universal essence, which is not wisdom, or love, or beauty, or power, but all in one, and each entirely, is that for which all things exist, and that by which they are; that spirit creates; that behind nature, throughout nature, spirit is present; one and not compound, it does not act upon us from without, that is, in space and time, but spiritually, or through ourselves: therefore, that spirit, that is, the Supreme Being, does not build up nature around us, but puts it forth through us, as the life of the tree puts forth new branches and leaves through the pores of the old. As a plant upon the earth, so a man rests upon the bosom of God; he is nourished by unfailing fountains, and draws at his need inexhaustible power. Who can set bounds to the possibilities of man? Once inhale the upper air, being admitted to behold the absolute natures of justice and truth, and we learn that man has access to the entire mind of the Creator, is himself the creator in the finite. This view, which admonishes me where the sources of wisdom and power lie, and points to virtue as to

> "The golden key
> Which opes the palace of eternity,"

carries upon its face the highest certificate of truth, because it animates me to create my own world through the purification of my soul.

The world proceeds from the same spirit as the body of man. It is a remoter and inferior incarnation of God, a projection of God in the unconscious. But it differs from the body in one important respect. It is not, like that, now subjected to the human will. Its serene order is inviolable by us. It is, therefore, to us, the present expositor of the divine mind. It is a fixed point whereby we may measure our departure. As we degenerate, the contrast between us and our house is more evident. We are as much strangers in nature as we are aliens from God. We do not understand the notes of birds. The fox and the deer run away from us; the bear and tiger rend us. We do not know the uses of more than a few plants, as corn and the apple, the potato and the vine. Is not the landscape, every glimpse of which hath a grandeur, a face of him? Yet this may show us what discord is between man and nature, for you cannot freely admire a noble landscape if laborers are digging in the field hard by. The poet finds something ridiculous in his delight until he is out of the sight of men.

VII   PROSPECTS

IN inquiries respecting the laws of the world and the frame of things, the highest reason is always the truest. That which seems faintly possible, it is so refined, is often faint and dim because it is deepest seated in the mind among the eternal verities. Empirical science is apt to cloud the sight, and, by the very knowledge of functions and processes, to bereave the student of the manly contemplation of the whole. The savant becomes unpoetic. But the best read naturalist who lends an entire and devout attention to truth, will see that there remains much to learn of his relation to the world, and that it is not to be learned by any addition or subtraction or other comparison of known quantities, but is arrived at by untaught sallies of the spirit, by a continual self-recovery, and by entire humility. He will perceive that there are far more excellent qualities in the student than preciseness and infallibility; that a guess is often more fruitful than an indisputable affirmation, and that a dream may let us deeper into the secret of nature than a hundred concerted experiments.

For the problems to be solved are precisely those which the physiologist and the naturalist omit to state. It is not so pertinent to man to know all the individuals of the animal kingdom, as it is to know whence and whereto is this tyrannizing unity in his constitution, which evermore separates and classifies things, endeavoring to reduce the most diverse to one form. When I behold a rich landscape, it is less to my purpose to recite correctly the order and superposition of the strata, than to know why all thought of multitude is lost in a tranquil sense of unity. I cannot greatly honor minuteness in details, so long as there is no hint to explain the relation between things and thoughts; no ray upon the *metaphysics* of conchology, of botany, of the arts, to show the relation of the forms of flowers, shells, animals, architecture, to the mind, and build science upon ideas. In a cabinet of natural history, we become sensible of a certain occult recognition and sympathy in regard to the most unwieldly and eccentric forms of beast, fish, and insect. The American who has been confined, in his own country, to the sight of buildings designed after foreign models, is surprised on entering York Minster or St. Peter's at Rome, by the feeling that these structures are imitations also,—faint copies of an invisible archetype. Nor has science sufficient humanity, so long as the naturalist overlooks that wonderful congruity which subsists between man and the world; of which he is lord, not because he is the most subtile inhabitant, but because he is its head and heart, and finds something of himself in every great and small thing, in every mountain stratum, in every new law of color, fact of astronomy, or atmospheric influence which observation or analysis lay open. A perception of this mystery inspires the muse of George Herbert, the beautiful psalmist of the seventeenth century. The following lines are part of his little poem on Man.

> Man is all symmetry,
> Full of proportions, one limb to another,
> And to all the world besides.
> Each part may call the farthest, brother;
> For head with foot hath private amity,
> And both with moons and tides.
>
> Nothing hath got so far
> But man hath caught and kept it as his prey;
> His eyes dismount the highest star;

He is in little all the sphere.
Herbs gladly cure our flesh, because that they
    Find their acquaintance there.

    For us, the winds do blow,
The earth doth rest, heaven move, and fountains flow;
    Nothing we see, but means our good,
    As our delight, or as our treasure;
The whole is either our cupboard of food,
    Or cabinet of pleasure.

    The stars have us to bed:
Night draws the curtain; which the sun withdraws.
    Music and light attend our head.
    All things unto our flesh are kind,
In their descent and being; to our mind,
    In their ascent and cause.

    More servants wait on man
Than he'll take notice of. In every path,
    He treads down that which doth befriend him
    When sickness makes him pale and wan.
Oh mighty love! Man is one world, and hath
    Another to attend him.

The perception of this class of truths makes the attraction which draws men to science, but the end is lost sight of in attention to the means. In view of this half-sight of science, we accept the sentence of Plato, that "poetry comes nearer to vital truth than history." Every surmise and vaticination of the mind is entitled to a certain respect, and we learn to prefer imperfect theories, and sentences, which contain glimpses of truth, to digested systems which have no one valuable suggestion. A wise writer will feel that the ends of study and composition are best answered by announcing undiscovered regions of thought, and so communicating, through hope, new activity to the torpid spirit.

I shall therefore conclude this essay with some traditions of man and nature, which a certain poet sang to me; and which, as they have always been in the world, and perhaps reappear to every bard, may be both history and prophecy.

'The foundations of man are not in matter, but in spirit. But the element of spirit is eternity. To it, therefore, the longest series of events, the oldest chronologies are young and recent. In the cycle of the universal man, from whom the known individuals proceed, centuries are points, and all history is but the epoch of one degradation.

'We distrust and deny inwardly our sympathy with nature. We own and disown our relation to it, by turns. We are like Nebuchadnezzar, dethroned, bereft of reason, and eating grass like an ox. But who can set limits to the remedial force of spirit?

'A man is a god in ruins. When men are innocent, life shall be longer, and shall pass into the immortal as gently as we awake from dreams. Now, the world would be insane and rabid, if these disorganizations should last for hundreds of years. It is kept in check by death and infancy. Infancy is the perpetual Messiah, which comes into the arms of fallen men, and pleads with them to return to paradise.

'Man is the dwarf of himself. Once he was permeated and dissolved by spirit. He filled nature with his overflowing currents. Out from him sprang the sun and moon; from man, the sun, from woman the moon. The laws of his mind, the periods of his actions externized themselves into day and night, into the year and the seasons. But, having made for himself this huge shell, his waters retired; he no longer fills the veins and veinlets; he is shrunk to a drop. He sees that the structure still fits him, but fits him colossally. Say, rather, once it fitted him, now it corresponds to him from far and on high. He adores timidly his own work. Now is man the follower of the sun, and woman the follower of the moon. Yet sometimes he starts in his slumber, and wonders at himself and his house, and muses strangely at the resemblance betwixt him and it. He perceives that if his law is still paramount, if still he have elemental power, if his word is sterling yet in nature, it is not conscious power, it is not inferior but superior to his will. It is Instinct.' Thus my Orphic poet sang.

At present, man applies to nature but half his force. He works on the world with his understanding alone. He lives in it and masters it by a penny-wisdom; and he that works most in it is but a half-man, and whilst his arms are strong and his digestion good, his mind is imbruted, and he is a selfish savage. His relation to nature, his power over it, is through the understanding; as by manure; the economic use of fire, wind, water, and the mariner's needle; steam, coal, chemical agriculture; the repairs of the human body by the dentist and the surgeon. This is such a resumption of power as if a banished king should buy his territories inch by inch, instead of vaulting at once into his throne. Meantime, in the thick darkness, there are not wanting gleams of a better light,—occasional examples of the action of man upon nature with his entire force,—with reason as well as understanding. Such examples are, the traditions of miracles in the earliest antiquity of all nations; the history of Jesus Christ; the achievements of a principle, as in religious and political revolutions, and in the abolition of the slave-trade; the miracles of enthusiasm, as those reported of Swedenborg, Hohenlohe, and the Shakers; many obscure and yet contested facts, now arranged under the name of Animal Magnetism; prayer; eloquence; self-healing; and the wisdom of children. These are examples of Reason's momentary grasp of the sceptre; the exertions of a power which exists not in time or space, but an instantaneous in-streaming causing power. The difference between the actual and the ideal force of man is happily figured by the schoolmen, in saying, that the knowledge of man is an evening knowledge, *vespertina cognitio*, but that of God is a morning knowledge, *matutina cognitio*.

The problem of restoring to the world original and eternal beauty is solved by the redemption of the soul. The ruin or the blank that we see when we look at nature, is in our own eye. The axis of vision is not coincident with the axis of things, and so they appear not transparent but opaque. The reason why the world lacks unity, and lies broken and in heaps, is because man is disunited with himself. He cannot be a naturalist until he satisfies all the demands of the spirit. Love is as much its demand as perception. Indeed, neither can be perfect without the other. In the uttermost meaning of the words, thought is devout, and devotion is thought. Deep calls unto deep. But in actual life, the marriage is not celebrated. There are innocent men who worship God after the tradition of their fathers, but their sense of duty has not yet extended to the use of all their faculties. And there are patient naturalists, but they freeze their subject under the wintry light of the understanding. Is not prayer also a study of truth,—a sally of the soul into the unfound infinite? No man ever prayed heartily without learning something. But when a faithful thinker, resolute to detach every object from personal relations and see it in the light of thought, shall, at the same time, kindle science with the fire of the holiest affections, then will God go forth anew into the creation.

It will not need, when the mind is prepared for study, to search for objects. The invariable mark of wisdom is to see the miraculous in the common. What is a day? What is a year? What is summer? What is woman? What is a child? What is sleep? To our blindness, these things seem unaffecting. We make fables to hide the baldness of the fact and conform it, as we say, to the higher law of the mind. But when the fact is seen under the light of an idea, the gaudy fable fades and shrivels. We behold the real higher law. To the wise, therefore, a fact is true poetry, and the most beautiful of fables. These wonders are brought to our own door. You also are a man. Man and woman and their social life, poverty, labor, sleep, fear, fortune, are known to you. Learn that none of these things is superficial, but that each phenomenon has its roots in the faculties and affections of the mind. Whilst the abstract question occupies your intellect, nature brings it in the concrete to be solved by your hands. It were a wise inquiry for the closet, to compare, point by point, especially at remarkable crises in life, our daily history with the rise and progress of ideas in the mind.

So shall we come to look at the world with new eyes. It shall answer the endless inquiry of the intellect,—What is truth? and of the affections,—What is good? by yielding itself passive to the educated Will. Then shall come to pass what my poet said; 'Nature is not fixed but fluid. Spirit alters, moulds, makes it. The immobility or bruteness of nature is the absence of spirit; to pure spirit it is fluid, it is volatile, it is obedient. Every spirit builds itself a house, and beyond its house a world, and beyond its world a heaven. Know then that the world exists for you. For you is the phenomenon perfect. What we are, that only can we see. All that Adam had, all that Caesar could, you have and can do. Adam called his house, heaven and earth; Caesar called his house, Rome; you perhaps call yours, a cobbler's trade; a hundred acres of ploughed land; or a scholar's garret. Yet line for line and point for point your dominion is as great as theirs, though without fine names. Build therefore your own world. As fast as you conform your life to the pure idea in your mind, that will unfold its great proportions. A correspondent revolution in things will attend the influx of the spirit. So fast will disagreeable appearances, swine, spiders, snakes, pests, mad-houses, prisons, enemies, vanish; they are temporary and shall be no more seen. The sordor and filths of nature, the sun shall dry up and the wind exhale. As when the summer comes from the south the snow-banks melt, and the face of the earth becomes green before it, so shall the advancing spirit create its ornaments along its path, and carry with it the beauty it visits, and the song which enchants it; it shall draw beautiful faces, warm hearts, wise discourse, and heroic acts, around its way, until evil is no more seen. The kingdom of man over nature, which cometh not with observation,—a dominion such as now is beyond his dream of God,—he shall enter without more wonder than the blind man feels who is gradually restored to perfect sight.'

'...*this yearning for the Wild*'

HENRY DAVID THOREAU

WALKING

1862

I WISH to speak a word for Nature, for absolute freedom and wildness, as contrasted with a freedom and culture merely civil—to regard man as an inhabitant, or a part and parcel of Nature, rather than a member of society. I wish to make an extreme statement, if so I may make an emphatic one, for there are enough champions of civilization: the minister and the school committee and every one of you will take care of that.

I have met with but one or two persons in the course of my life who understood the art of Walking, that is, of taking walks—who had a genius, so to speak, for *sauntering*, which word is beautifully derived "from idle people who roved about the country, in the Middle Ages, and asked charity, under pretense of going *à la Sainte Terre*," to the Holy Land, till the children exclaimed, "There goes a *Sainte-Terrer*," a Saunterer, a Holy-Lander. They who never go to the Holy Land in their walks, as they pretend, are indeed mere idlers and vagabonds; but they who do go there are saunterers in the good sense, such as I mean. Some, however, would derive the word from *sans terre* without land or a home, which, therefore, in the good sense, will mean, having no particular home, but equally at home everywhere. For this is the secret of successful sauntering. He who sits still in a house all the time may be the greatest vagrant of all; but the saunterer, in the good sense, is no more vagrant than the meandering river, which is all the while sedulously seeking the shortest course to the sea. But I prefer the first, which, indeed, is the most probable derivation. For every walk is a sort of crusade, preached by some Peter the Hermit in us, to go forth and reconquer this Holy Land from the hands of the Infidels.

It is true, we are but faint-hearted crusaders, even the walkers, nowadays, who undertake no persevering, never-ending enterprises. Our expeditions are but tours, and come round again at evening to the old hearthside from which we set out. Half the walk is but retracing our steps. We should go forth on the shortest walk, perchance, in the spirit of undying adventure, never to return, prepared to send back our embalmed hearts only as relics to our desolate kingdoms. If you are ready to leave father and mother, and brother and sister, and wife and child and friends, and never see them again—if you have paid your debts, and made your will, and settled all your affairs, and are a free man—then you are ready for a walk.

To come down to my own experience, my companion and I, for I sometimes have a companion, take pleasure in fancying ourselves knights of a new, or rather an old, order—not Equestrians or Chevaliers, not Ritters or Riders, but Walkers, a still more ancient and honorable class, I trust. The chivalric and heroic spirit which once belonged to the Rider seems now to reside in, or perchance to have subsided into, the Walker—not the Knight, but Walker, Errant. He is a sort of fourth estate, outside of Church and State and People.

We have felt that we almost alone hereabouts practiced this noble art; though, to tell the truth, at least if their own assertions are to be received, most of my townsmen would fain walk sometimes, as I do, but they cannot. No wealth can buy the requisite leisure, freedom, and independence which are the capital in this profession. It comes only by the grace of God. It requires a direct dispensation from Heaven to become a walker. You must be born into the family of the Walkers. *Ambulator nascitur, non fit.* Some of my townsmen, it is true, can remember and have described to me some walks which they took ten years ago, in which they were so blessed as to lose themselves for half an hour in the woods; but I know very well that they have confined themselves to the highway ever since, whatever pretensions they may make to belong to this select class. No doubt they were elevated for a moment as by the reminiscence of a previous state of existence, when even they were foresters and outlaws.

> "When he came to grene wode,
> In a mery mornynge,
> There he herde the notes small
> Of byrdes mery syngynge.
>
> "It is ferre gone, sayd Robyn,
> That I was last here;
> Me Lyste a lytell for to shote
> At the donne dere."

I think that I cannot preserve my health and spirits, unless I spend four hours a day at least—and it is commonly more than that—sauntering through the woods and over the hills and fields, absolutely free from all worldly engagements. You may safely say, A penny for your thoughts, or a thousand pounds. When sometimes I am reminded that the mechanics and shopkeepers stay in their shops not only all the forenoon, but all the afternoon too, sitting with crossed legs, so many of them—as if the legs were made to sit upon, and not to stand or walk upon—I think that they deserve some credit for not having all committed suicide long ago.

I, who cannot stay in my chamber for a single day without acquiring some rust, and when sometimes I have stolen forth for a walk at the eleventh hour, or four o'clock in the afternoon, too late to redeem the day, when the shades of night were already beginning to be mingled with the daylight, have felt as if I had committed some sin to be atoned for—I confess that I am astonished at the power of endurance, to say nothing of the moral insensibility, of my neighbors who confine themselves to shops and offices the whole day for weeks and months, aye, and years almost together. I know not what manner of stuff they are of, sitting there now at three o'clock in the afternoon, as if it were three o'clock in the morning. Bonaparte may talk of the three-o'clock-in-the-morning courage, but it is nothing to the courage which can sit down cheerfully at this hour in the afternoon over against one's self whom you have known all the morning, to starve out a garrison to whom you are bound by such strong ties of sympathy. I wonder that about this time, or say between four and five o'clock in the afternoon, too late for the morning papers and too early for the evening ones, there is not a general explosion heard up and down the street, scattering a legion of antiquated and house-bred notions and whims to the four winds for an airing—and so the evil cure itself.

How womankind, who are confined to the house still more than men, stand it I do not know; but I have ground to suspect that most of them do not *stand* it at all. When, early in a summer afternoon, we have been shaking the dust of the village from the skirts of our garments, making haste past those houses with purely Doric or Gothic fronts, which have such an air of repose about them, my companion whispers that probably about these times their occupants are all gone to bed. Then it is that I appreciate the beauty and the glory of architecture, which itself never turns in, but forever stands out and erect, keeping watch over the slumberers.

No doubt temperament, and, above all, age, have a good deal to do with it. As a man grows older, his ability to sit still and follow indoor occupations increases. He grows vespertinal in his habits as the evening of life approaches, till at last he comes forth only just before sundown, and gets all the walk that he requires in half an hour.

But the walking of which I speak has nothing in it akin to taking exercise, as it is called, as the sick take medicine at stated hours—as the swinging of dumbbells or chairs; but is itself the enterprise and adventure of the day. If you would get exercise, go in search of the springs of life. Think of a man's swinging dumbbells for his health, when those springs are bubbling up in far-off pastures unsought by him!

Moreover, you must walk like a camel, which is said to be the only beast which ruminates when walking. When a traveler asked Wordsworth's servant to show him her master's study, she answered, "Here is his library, but his study is out of doors."

Living much out of doors, in the sun and wind, will no doubt produce a certain roughness of character—will cause a thicker cuticle to grow over some of the finer qualities of our nature, as on the face and hands, or as severe manual labor robs the hands of some of their delicacy of touch. So staying in the house, on the other hand, may produce a softness and smoothness, not to say thinness of skin, accompanied by an increased sensibility to certain impressions. Perhaps we should be more susceptible to some influences important to our intellectual and moral growth, if the sun had shone and the wind blown on us a little less; and no doubt it is a nice matter to proportion rightly the thick and thin skin. But methinks that is a scurf that will fall off fast enough—that the natural remedy is to be found in the proportion which the night bears to the day, the winter to the summer, thought to experience. There will be so much the more air and sunshine in our thoughts. The callous palms of the laborer are conversant with finer tissues of self-respect and heroism, whose touch thrills the heart, than the languid fingers of idleness. That is mere sentimentality that lies abed by day and thinks itself white, far from the tan and callus of experience.

When we walk, we naturally go to the fields and woods: what would become of us, if we walked only in a garden or a mall? Even some sects of philosophers have felt the necessity of importing the woods to themselves, since they did not go to the woods. "They planted groves and walks of Platanes," where they took *subdiales ambulationes* in porticos open to the air. Of course it is of no use to direct our steps to the woods, if they do not carry us thither. I am alarmed when it happens that I have walked a mile into the woods bodily, without getting there in spirit. In my afternoon walk I would fain forget all my morning occupations and my obligations to society. But it sometimes happens that I cannot easily shake off the village. The thought of some work will run in my head and I am not where my body is—I am out of my senses. In my walks I would fain return to my senses. What business have I in the woods, if I am thinking of something out of the woods? I suspect myself, and cannot help a shudder, when I find myself so implicated even in what are called good works—for this may sometimes happen.

My vicinity affords many good walks; and though for so many years I have walked almost every day, and sometimes for several days together, I have not yet exhausted them. An absolutely new prospect is a great happiness, and I can still get this any afternoon. Two or three hours' walking will carry me to as strange a country as I expect ever to see. A single farmhouse which I had not seen before is sometimes as good as the dominions of the King of Dahomey. There is in fact a sort of harmony discoverable between the capabilities of the landscape within a circle of ten miles' radius, or the limits of an afternoon walk, and the threescore years and ten of human life. It will never become quite familiar to you.

Nowadays almost all man's improvements, so called, as the building of houses and the cutting down of the forest and of all large trees, simply deform the landscape, and make it more and more tame and cheap. A people who would begin by burning the fences and let the forest stand! I saw the fences half consumed, their ends lost in the middle of the prairie, and some worldly miser with a surveyor looking after his bounds, while heaven had taken place around him, and he did not see the angels going to and fro, but was looking for an old post-hole in the midst of paradise. I looked again, and saw him standing in the middle of a boggy Stygian fen, surrounded by devils, and he had found his bounds without a doubt, three little stones, where a stake had been driven, and looking nearer, I saw that the Prince of Darkness was his surveyor.

I can easily walk ten, fifteen, twenty, any number of miles, commencing at my own door, without going by any house, without crossing a road except where the fox and the mink do: first along by the river, and then the brook, and then the meadow and the woodside. There are square miles in my vicinity which have no inhabitant. From many a hill I can see civilization and the abodes of man afar. The farmers and their works are scarcely more obvious than woodchucks and their burrows. Man and his affairs, church and state and school, trade and commerce, and manufactures and agriculture, even politics, the most alarming of them all—I am pleased to see how little space they occupy in the landscape. Politics is but a narrow field, and that still narrower highway yonder leads to it. I sometimes direct the traveler thither. If you would go to the political world, follow the great road, follow that market-man, keep his dust in your eyes, and it will lead you straight to it; for it, too, has its place merely, and does not occupy all space. I pass from it as from a bean field into the forest, and it is forgotten. In one half-hour I can walk off to some portion of the earth's surface where a man does not stand from one year's end to another, and there, consequently, politics are not, for they are but as the cigar-smoke of a man.

The village is the place to which the roads tend, a sort of expansion of the highway, as a lake of a river. It is the body of which roads are the arms and legs—a trivial or quadrivial place, the thoroughfare and ordinary of travelers. The word is from the Latin *villa*, which together with *via*, a way, or more anciently *ved* and *vella*, Varro derives from *veho*, to carry, because the villa is the place to and from which things are carried. They who got their living by teaming were said *vellaturam facere*. Hence, too, the Latin word *vilis* and our vile, also *villain*. This suggests what kind of degeneracy villagers are liable to. They are wayworn by the travel that goes by and over them, without traveling themselves.

Some do not walk at all; others walk in the highways; a few walk across lots. Roads are made for horses and men of business. I do not travel in them much, comparatively, because I am not in a hurry to get to any tavern or grocery or livery-stable or depot to which they lead. I am a good horse to travel, but not from choice a roadster. The landscape-painter uses the figures of men to mark a road. He would not make that use of my figure. I walk out into a nature such as the old prophets and poets, Menu, Moses, Homer, Chaucer, walked in. You may name it America, but it is not America; neither Americus Vespucius, nor Columbus, nor the rest were the discoverers of it. There is a truer account of it in mythology than in any history of America, so called, that I have seen.

However, there are a few old roads that may be trodden with profit, as if they led somewhere now that they are nearly discontinued. There is the Old Marlborough Road, which does not go to Marlborough now, methinks, unless that is Marlborough where it carries me. I am the bolder to speak of it here, because I presume that there are one or two such roads in every town.

THE OLD MALBOROUGH ROAD

Where they once dug for money,
But never found any;
Where sometimes Martial Miles
Singly files,
And Elijah Wood,
I fear for no good:
No other man,
Save Elisha Dugan—
O man of wild habits,
Partridges and rabbits
Who hast no cares
Only to set snares,
Who liv'st all alone,
Close to the bone,
And where life is sweetest
Constantly eatest.
When the spring stirs my blood
   With the instinct to travel,
   I can get enough gravel
On the Old Marlborough Road.
   Nobody repairs it,
   For nobody wears it;
   It is a living way,
   As the Christians say.
Not many there be
  Who enter therein,
Only the guests of the
  Irishman Quin.
What is it, what is it
  But a direction out there,
And the bare possibility
  Of going somewhere?
   Great guide-boards of stone,

But travelers none;
Cenotaphs of the towns
Named on their crowns.
It is worth going to see
Where you *might* be.
What king
Did the thing,
I am still wondering;
Set up how or when,
By what selectmen,
Gourgas or Lee,
Clark or Darby?
They're a great endeavor
To be something forever;
Blank tablets of stone,
Where a traveler might groan,
And in one sentence
Grave all that is known;
Which another might read,
In his extreme need.
I know one or two
Lines that would do,
Literature that might stand
All over the land,
Which a man could remember
Till next December,
And read again in the spring,
After the thawing.
If with fancy unfurled
  You leave your abode,
You may go round the world
   By the Old Marlborough Road.

At present, in this vicinity, the best part of the land is not private property; the landscape is not owned, and the walker enjoys comparative freedom. But possibly the day will come when it will be partitioned off into so-called pleasure-grounds, in which a few will take a narrow and exclusive pleasure only—when fences shall be multiplied, and man-traps and other engines invented to confine men to the *public* road, and walking over the surface of God's earth shall be construed to mean trespassing on some gentleman's grounds. To enjoy a thing exclusively is commonly to exclude yourself from the true enjoyment of it. Let us improve our opportunities, then, before the evil days come.

What is it that makes it so hard sometimes to determine whither we will walk? I believe that there is a subtle magnetism in Nature, which, if we unconsciously yield to it, will direct us aright. It is not indifferent to us which way we walk. There is a right way; but we are very liable from heedlessness and stupidity to take the wrong one. We would fain take that walk, never yet taken by us through this actual world, which is perfectly symbolical of the path which we love to travel in the interior and ideal world; and sometimes, no doubt, we find it difficult to choose our direction, because it does not yet exist distinctly in our idea.

When I go out of the house for a walk, uncertain as yet whither I will bend my steps, and submit myself to my instinct to decide for me, I find, strange and whimsical as it may seem, that I finally and inevitably settle southwest, toward some particular wood or meadow or deserted pasture or hill in that direction. My needle is slow to settle, varies a few degrees, and does not always point due southwest, it is true, and it has good authority for this variation, but it always settles between west and south-southwest. The future lies that way to me, and the earth seems more unexhausted and richer on that side. The outline which would bound my walks would be, not a circle, but a parabola, or rather like one of those cometary orbits which have been thought to be non-returning curves, in this case opening westward, in which my house occupies the place of the sun. I turn round and round irresolute sometimes for a quarter of an hour, until I decide, for a thousandth time, that I will walk into the southwest or west. Eastward I go only by force; but westward I go free. Thither no business leads me. It is hard for me to believe that I shall find fair landscapes or sufficient wildness and freedom behind the eastern horizon. I am not excited by the prospect of a walk thither; but I believe that the forest which I see in the western horizon stretches uninterruptedly toward the setting sun, and there are no towns nor cities in it of enough consequence to disturb me. Let me live where I will, on this side is the city, on that the wilderness, and ever I am leaving the city more and more, and withdrawing into the wilderness. I should not lay so much stress on this fact, if I did not believe that something like this is the prevailing tendency of my countrymen. I must walk toward Oregon, and not toward Europe. And that way the nation is moving, and I may say that mankind progress from east to west. Within a few years we have witnessed the phenomenon of a southeastward migration, in the settlement of Australia; but this affects us as a retrograde movement, and, judging from the moral and physical character of the first generation of Australians, has not yet proved a successful experiment. The eastern Tartars think that there is nothing west beyond Thibet. "The world ends there," say they; "beyond there is nothing but a shoreless sea." It is unmitigated East where they live.

We go eastward to realize history and study the works of art and literature, retracing the steps of the race; we go westward as into the future, with a spirit of enterprise and adventure. The Atlantic is a Lethean stream, in our passage over which we have had an opportunity to forget the Old World and its institutions. If we do not succeed this time, there is perhaps one more chance for the race left before it arrives on the banks of the Styx; and that is in the Lethe of the Pacific, which is three times as wide.

I know not how significant it is, or how far it is an evidence of singularity, that an individual should thus consent in his pettiest walk with the general movement of the race; but I know that something akin to the migratory instinct in birds and quadrupeds—which, in some instances, is known to have affected the squirrel tribe, impelling them to a general and mysterious movement, in which they were seen, say some, crossing the broadest rivers, each on its particular chip, with its tail raised for a sail, and bridging narrower streams with their dead—that something like the *furor* which affects the domestic cattle in the spring, and which is referred to a worm in their tails, affects both nations and individuals, either perennially or from time to time. Not a flock of wild geese cackles over our town, but it to some extent unsettles the value of real estate here, and, if I were a broker, I should probably take that disturbance into account.

> "Than longen folk to gon on pilgrimages,
> And palmeres for to seken strange strondes."

Every sunset which I witness inspires me with the desire to go to a West as distant and as fair as that into which the sun goes down. He appears to migrate westward daily, and tempt us to follow him. He is the Great Western Pioneer whom the nations follow. We dream all night of those mountain-ridges in the horizon, though they may be of vapor only, which were last gilded by his rays. The island of Atlantis, and the islands and gardens of the Hesperides, a sort of terrestrial paradise, appear to have been the Great West of the ancients, enveloped in mystery and poetry. Who has not seen in imagination, when looking into the sunset sky, the gardens of the Hesperides, and the foundation of all those fables?

Columbus felt the westward tendency more strongly than any before. He obeyed it, and found a New World for Castile and Leon. The herd of men in those days scented fresh pastures from afar,

> "And now the sun had stretched out all the hills,
> And now was dropped into the western bay;
> At last *he* rose, and twitched his mantle blue;
> Tomorrow to fresh woods and pastures new."

Where on the globe can there be found an area of equal extent with that occupied by the bulk of our States, so fertile and so rich and varied in its productions, and at the same time so habitable by the European, as this is? Michaux, who knew but part of them, says that "the species of large trees are much more numerous in North America than in Europe; in the United States there are more than one hundred and forty species that exceed thirty feet in height; in France there are but thirty that attain this size." Later botanists more than confirm his observations. Humboldt came to America to realize his youthful dreams of a tropical vegetation, and he beheld it in its greatest perfection in the primitive forests of the Amazon, the most gigantic wilderness on the earth, which he has so eloquently described. The geographer Guyot, himself a European, goes farther—farther than I am ready to follow him; yet not when he says: "As the plant is made for the animal, as the vegetable world is made for the animal world, America is made for the man of the Old World.... The man of the Old World sets out upon his way. Leaving the highlands of Asia, he descends from station to station towards Europe. Each of his steps is marked by a new civilization superior to the preceding, by a greater power of development. Arrived at the Atlantic, he pauses on the shore of this unknown ocean, the bounds of which he knows not, and turns upon his footprints for an instant." When he has exhausted the rich soil of Europe, and reinvigorated himself, "then recommences his adventurous career westward as in the earliest ages." So far Guyot.

From this western impulse coming in contact with the barrier of the Atlantic sprang the commerce and enterprise of modern times. The younger Michaux, in his *Travels West of the Alleghanies in 1802*, says that the common inquiry in the newly settled West was, " 'From what part of the world have you come?' As if these vast and fertile regions would naturally be the place of meeting and common country of all the inhabitants of the globe."

To use an obsolete Latin word, I might say, *Ex Oriente lux; ex Occidente* FRUX. From the East light; from the West fruit.

Sir Francis Head, an English traveler and a Governor-General of Canada, tells us that "in both the northern and southern hemispheres of the New World, Nature has not only outlined her works on a larger scale, but has painted the whole picture with brighter, and more costly colors than she used in delineating and in beautifying the Old World....The heavens of America appear infinitely higher, the sky is bluer, the air is fresher, the cold is intenser, the moon looks larger, the stars are brighter, the thunder is louder, the lightning is vivider, the wind is stronger, the rain is heavier, the mountains are higher, the rivers longer, the forests bigger, the plains broader." This statement will do at least to set against Buffon's account of this part of the world and its productions.

Linnaeus said long ago, "*Nescio quae facies* laeta, glabra *plantis Americanis*" (I know not what there is of joyous and smooth in the aspect of American plants); and I think that in this country there are no, or at most very few, *Africanae bestiae*, African beasts, as the Romans called them, and that in this respect also it is peculiarly fitted for the habitation of man. We are told that within three miles of the center of the East-Indian city of Singapore, some of the inhabitants are annually carried off by tigers; but the traveler can lie down in the woods at night almost anywhere in North America without fear of wild beasts.

These are encouraging testimonies. If the moon looks larger here than in Europe, probably the sun looks larger also. If the heavens of America appear infinitely higher, and the stars brighter, I trust that these facts are symbolical of the height to which the philosophy and poetry and religion of her inhabitants may one day soar. At length, perchance, the immaterial heaven will appear as much higher to the American mind, and the intimations that star it as much brighter. For I believe that climate does thus react on man—as there is something in the mountain air that feeds the spirit and inspires. Will not man grow to greater perfection intellectually as well as physically under these influences? Or is it unimportant how many foggy days there are in his life? I trust that we shall be more imaginative, that our thoughts will be clearer, fresher, and more ethereal, as our sky—our understanding more comprehensive and broader, like our plains—our intellect generally on a grander scale, like our thunder and lightning, our rivers and mountains and forests—and our hearts shall even correspond in breadth and depth and grandeur to our inland seas. Perchance there will appear to the traveler something, he knows not what, of *laeta* and *glabra*, of joyous and serene, in our very faces. Else to what end does the world go on, and why was America discovered?

> To Americans I hardly need to say,
> "Westward the star of empire takes its way."

As a true patriot, I should be ashamed to think that Adam in paradise was more favorably situated on the whole than the backwoodsman in this country.

Our sympathies in Massachusetts are not confined to New England; though we may be estranged from the South, we sympathize with the West. There is the home of the younger sons, as among the Scandinavians they took to the sea for their inheritance. It is too late to be studying Hebrew; it is more important to understand even the slang of today.

Some months ago I went to see a panorama of the Rhine. It was like a dream of the Middle Ages. I floated down its historic stream in something more than imagination, under bridges built by the Romans, and repaired by later heroes, past cities and castles whose very names were music to my ears, and each of which was the subject of a legend. There were Ehrenbreitstein and Rolandseck and Coblentz, which I knew only in history. They were ruins that interested me chiefly. There seemed to come up from its waters and its vine-clad hills and valleys a hushed music as of Crusaders departing for the Holy Land. I floated along under the spell of enchantment, as if I had been transported to an heroic age, and breathed an atmosphere of chivalry.

Soon after, I went to see a panorama of the Mississippi, and as I worked my way up the river in the light of today, and saw the steamboats wooding up, counted the rising cities, gazed on the fresh ruins of Nauvoo, beheld the Indians moving west across the stream, and, as before I had looked up the Moselle, now looked up the Ohio and the Missouri and heard the legends of Dubuque and of Wenona's Cliff—still thinking more of the future than of the past or present—I saw that this was a Rhine stream of a different kind; that the foundations of castles were yet to be laid, and the famous bridges were yet to be thrown over the river; and I felt that *this was the heroic age itself*, though we know it not, for the hero is commonly the simplest and obscurest of men.

The West of which I speak is but another name for the Wild; and what I have been preparing to say is, that in Wildness is the preservation of the World. Every tree sends its fibers forth in search of the Wild. The cities import it at any price. Men plow and sail for it. From the forest and wilderness come the tonics and barks which brace mankind. Our ancestors were savages. The story of Romulus and Remus being suckled by a wolf is not a meaningless fable. The founders of every state which has risen to eminence have drawn their nourishment and vigor from a similar wild source. It was because the children of the Empire were not suckled by the wolf that they were conquered and displaced by the children of the northern forests who were.

I believe in the forest, and in the meadow, and in the night in which the corn grows. We require an infusion of hemlock, spruce or arbor vitae in our tea. There is a difference between eating and drinking for strength and from mere gluttony. The Hottentots eagerly devour the marrow of the koodoo and other antelopes raw, as a matter of course. Some of our northern Indians eat raw the marrow of the Arctic reindeer, as well as various other parts, including the summits of the antlers, as long as they are soft. And herein, perchance, they have stolen a march on the cooks of Paris. They get what usually goes to feed the fire. This is probably better than stall-fed beef and slaughterhouse pork to make a man of. Give me a wildness whose glance no civilization can endure—as if we lived on the marrow of koodoos devoured raw.

There are some intervals which border the strain of the wood thrush, to which I would migrate—wild lands where no settler has squatted; to which, methinks, I am already acclimated.

The African hunter Cumming tells us that the skin of the eland, as well as that of most other antelopes just killed, emits the most delicious perfume of trees and grass. I would have every man so much like a wild antelope, so much a part and parcel of nature, that his very person should thus sweetly advertise our senses of his presence, and remind us of those parts of nature which he most haunts. I feel no disposition to the satirical, when the trapper's coat emits the odor of musquash even; it is a sweeter scent to me than that which commonly exhales from the merchant's or the scholar's garments. When I go into their wardrobes and handle their vestments, I am reminded of no grassy plains and flowery meads which they have frequented, but of dusty merchants' exchanges and libraries rather.

A tanned skin is something more than respectable, and perhaps olive is a fitter color than white for a man—a denizen of the woods. "The pale white man!" I do not wonder that the African pitied him. Darwin the naturalist says, "A white man bathing by the side of a Tahitian was like a plant bleached by the gardener's art, compared with a fine, dark green one, growing vigorously in the open fields."

Ben Jonson exclaims,—

"How near to good is what is fair!"

So I would say,

"How near to good is what is *wild*!"

Life consists with wildness. The most alive is the wildest. Not yet subdued to man, its presence refreshes him. One who pressed forward incessantly and never rested from his labors, who grew fast and made infinite demands on life, would always find himself in a new country or wilderness, and surrounded by the raw material of life. He would be climbing over the prostrate stems of primitive forest-trees.

Hope and the future for me are not in lawns and cultivated fields, not in towns and cities, but in the impervious and quaking swamps. When, formerly, I have analyzed my partiality for some farm which I had contemplated purchasing, I have frequently found that I was attracted solely by a few square rods of impermeable and unfathomable bog—a natural sink in one corner of it. That was the jewel which dazzled me. I derive more of my subsistence from the swamps which surround my native town than from the cultivated gardens in the village. There are no richer parterres to my eyes than the dense beds of dwarf andromeda (*Cassandra calyculata*) which cover these tender places on the earth's surface. Botany cannot go farther than tell me the names of the shrubs which grow there—the high blueberry, panicled andromeda, lambkill, azalea, and rhodora—all standing in the quaking sphagnum. I often think that I should like to have my house front on this mass of dull red bushes, omitting other flower plots and borders, transplanted spruce and trim box, even graveled walks—to have this fertile spot under my windows, not a few imported barrowfuls of soil only to cover the sand which was thrown out in digging the cellar. Why not put my house, my parlor, behind this plot, instead of behind that meager assemblage of curiosities, that poor apology for a Nature and Art, which I call my front yard? It is an effort to clear up and make a decent appearance when the carpenter and mason have departed, though done as much for the passer-by as the dweller within. The most tasteful front-yard fence was never an agreeable object of study to me; the most elaborate ornaments, acorn tops, or what not, soon wearied and disgusted me. Bring your sills up to the very edge of the swamp, then (though it may not be the best place for a dry cellar), so that there be no access on that side to citizens. Front yards are not made to walk in, but, at most, through, and you could go in the back way.

Yes, though you may think me perverse, if it were proposed to me to dwell in the neighborhood of the most beautiful garden that ever human art contrived, or else of a Dismal Swamp, I should certainly decide for the swamp. How vain, then, have been all your labors, citizens, for me!

My spirits infallibly rise in proportion to the outward dreariness. Give me the ocean, the desert, or the wilderness! In the desert, pure air and solitude compensate for want of moisture and fertility. The traveler Burton says of it: "Your *morale* improves; you become frank and cordial, hospitable and single-minded....In the desert, spirituous liquors excite only disgust. There is a keen enjoyment in a mere animal existence." They who have been traveling long on the steppes of Tartary say, "On re-entering cultivated lands, the agitation, perplexity, and turmoil of civilization oppressed and suffocated us; the air seemed to fail us, and we felt every moment as if about to die of asphyxia." When I would recreate myself, I seek the darkest wood, the thickest and most interminable and, to the citizen, most dismal, swamp. I enter a swamp as a sacred place, a *sanctum sanctorum*. There is the strength, the marrow, of Nature. The wildwood covers the virgin mould, and the same soil is good for men and for trees. A man's health requires as many acres of meadow to his prospect as his farm does loads of muck. There are the strong meats on which he feeds. A town is saved, not more by the righteous men in it than by the woods and swamps that surround it. A township where one primitive forest waves above while another primitive forest rots below—such a town is fitted to raise not only corn and potatoes, but poets and philosophers for the coming ages. In such a soil grew Homer and Confucius and the rest, and out of such a wilderness comes the Reformer eating locusts and wild honey.

To preserve wild animals implies generally the creation of a forest for them to dwell in or resort to. So it is with man. A hundred years ago they sold bark in our streets peeled from our own woods. In the very aspect of those primitive and rugged trees there was, methinks, a tanning principle which hardened and consolidated the fibers of men's thoughts. Ah! already I shudder for these comparatively degenerate days of my native village, when you cannot collect a load of bark of good thickness, and we no longer produce tar and turpentine.

The civilized nations—Greece, Rome, England—have been sustained by the primitive forests which anciently rotted where they stand. They survive as long as the soil is not exhausted. Alas for human culture! little is to be expected of a nation, when the vegetable mould is exhausted, and it is compelled to make manure of the bones of its fathers. There the poet sustains himself merely by his own superfluous fat, and the philosopher comes down on his marrow-bones.

It is said to be the task of the American "to work the virgin soil," and that "agriculture here already assumes proportions unknown everywhere else." I think that the farmer displaces the Indian even because he redeems the meadow, and so makes himself stronger and in some respects more natural. I was surveying for a man the other day a single straight line one hundred and thirty-two rods long, through a swamp at whose entrance might have been written the words which Dante read over the entrance to the infernal regions, "Leave all hope, ye that enter"—that is, of ever getting out again; where at one time I saw my employer actually up to his neck and swimming for his life in his property, though it was still winter. He had another similar swamp which I could not survey at all, because it was completely under water, and nevertheless, with regard to a third swamp, which I did *survey* from a distance, he remarked to me, true to his instincts, that he would not part with it for any consideration, on account of the mud which it contained. And that man intends to put a girdling ditch round the whole in the course of forty months, and so redeem it by the magic of his spade. I refer to him only as the type of a class.

The weapons with which we have gained our most important victories, which should be handed down as heirlooms from father to son, are not the sword and the lance, but the bushwhack, the turf-cutter, the spade, and the bog hoe, rusted with the blood of many a meadow, and begrimed with the dust of many a hard-fought field. The very winds blew the Indian's cornfield into the meadow, and pointed out the way which he had not the skill to follow. He had no better implement with which to intrench himself in the land than a clam-shell. But the farmer is armed with plow and spade.

In literature it is only the wild that attracts us. Dullness is but another name for tameness. It is the uncivilized free and wild thinking in Hamlet and the Iliad, in all the scriptures and mythologies, not learned in the schools, that delights us. As the wild duck is more swift and beautiful than the tame, so is the wild—the mallard—thought, which 'mid falling dews wings its way above the fens. A truly good book is something as natural, and as unexpectedly and unaccountably fair and perfect, as a wild-flower discovered on the prairies of the West or in the jungles of the East. Genius is a light which makes the darkness visible, like the lightning's flash, which perchance shatters the temple of knowledge itself—and not a taper lighted at the hearthstone of the race, which pales before the light of common day.

English literature, from the days of the minstrels to the Lake Poets—Chaucer and Spenser and Milton, and even Shakespeare, included—breathes no quite fresh and, in this sense, wild strain. It is an essentially tame and civilized literature, reflecting Greece and Rome. Her wilderness is a greenwood, her wild man a Robin Hood. There is plenty of genial love of Nature, but not so much of Nature herself. Her chronicles inform us when her wild animals, but not when the wild man in her, became extinct.

The science of Humboldt is one thing, poetry is another thing. The poet today, notwithstanding all the discoveries of science, and the accumulated learning of mankind, enjoys no advantage over Homer.

Where is the literature which gives expression to Nature? He would be a poet who could impress the winds and streams into his service, to speak for him; who nailed words to their primitive senses, as farmers drive down stakes in the spring, which the frost has heaved; who derived his words as often as he used them—transplanted them to his page with earth adhering to their roots; whose words were so true and fresh and natural that they would appear to expand like the buds at the approach of spring, though they lay half smothered between two musty leaves in a library—aye, to bloom and bear fruit there, after their kind, annually, for the faithful reader, in sympathy with surrounding Nature.

I do not know of any poetry to quote which adequately expresses this yearning for the Wild. Approached from this side, the best poetry is tame. I do not know where to find in any literature, ancient or modern, any account which contents me of that Nature with which even I am acquainted. You will perceive that I demand something which no Augustan nor Elizabethan age, which no *culture*, in short, can give. Mythology comes nearer to it than anything. How much more fertile a Nature, at least, has Grecian mythology its root in than English literature! Mythology is the crop which the Old World bore before its soil was exhausted, before the fancy and imagination were affected with blight; and which it still bears, wherever its pristine vigor is unabated. All other literatures endure only as the elms which overshadow our houses; but this is like the great dragon-tree of the Western Isles, as old as mankind, and, whether that does or not, will endure as long; for the decay of other literatures makes the soil in which it thrives.

The West is preparing to add its fables to those of the East. The valleys of the Ganges, the Nile, and the Rhine having yielded their crop, it remains to be seen what the valleys of the Amazon, the Plate, the Orinoco, the St. Lawrence, and the Mississippi will produce. Perchance, when, in the course of ages, American liberty has become a fiction of the past—as it is to some extent a fiction of the present—the poets of the world will be inspired by American mythology.

The wildest dreams of wild men, even, are not the less true, though they may not recommend themselves to the sense which is most common among Englishmen and Americans today. It is not every truth that recommends itself to the common sense. Nature has a place for the wild clematis as well as for the cabbage. Some expressions of truth are reminiscent, others merely *sensible*, as the phrase is, others prophetic. Some forms of disease, even, may prophesy forms of health. The geologist has discovered that the figures of serpents, griffins, flying dragons, and other fanciful embellishments of heraldry, have their prototypes in the forms of fossil species which were extinct before man was created, and hence "indicate a faint and shadowy knowledge of a previous state of organic existence." The Hindus dreamed that the earth rested on an elephant, and the elephant on a tortoise, and the tortoise on a serpent; and though it may be an unimportant coincidence, it will not be out of place here to state, that a fossil tortoise has lately been discovered in Asia large enough to support an elephant. I confess that I am partial to these wild fancies, which transcend the order of time and development. They are the sublimest recreation of the intellect. The partridge loves peas, but not those that go with her into the pot.

In short, all good things are wild and free. There is something in a strain of music, whether produced by an instrument or by the human voice—take the sound of a bugle in a summer night, for instance—which by its wildness, to speak without satire, reminds me of the cries emitted by wild beasts in their native forests. It is so much of their wildness as I can understand. Give me for my friends and neighbors wild men, not tame ones. The wildness of the savage is but a faint symbol of the awful ferity with which good men and lovers meet.

I love even to see the domestic animals reassert their native rights—any evidence that they have not wholly lost their original wild habits and vigor; as when my neighbor's cow breaks out of her pasture early in the spring and boldly swims the river, a cold, gray tide, twenty-five or thirty rods wide, swollen by the melted snow. It is the buffalo crossing the Mississippi. This exploit confers some dignity on the herd in my eyes—already dignified. The seeds of instinct are preserved under the thick hides of cattle and horses, like seeds in the bowels of the earth, an indefinite period.

Any sportiveness in cattle is unexpected. I saw one day a herd of a dozen bullocks and cows running about and frisking in unwieldy sport, like huge rats, even like kittens. They shook their heads, raised their tails, and rushed up and down a hill, and I perceived by their horns, as well as by their activity, their relation to the deer tribe. But, alas! a sudden loud *Whoa*! would have damped their ardor at once, reduced them from venison to beef, and stiffened their sides and sinews like the locomotive. Who but the Evil One has cried "Whoa!" to mankind? Indeed, the life of cattle, like that of many men, is but a sort of locomotiveness; they move a side at a time, and man, by his machinery, is meeting the horse and the ox halfway. Whatever part the whip has touched is thenceforth palsied. Who would ever think of a *side* of any of the supple cat tribe, as we speak of a *side* of beef?

I rejoice that horses and steers have to be broken before they can be made the slaves of men, and that men themselves have some wild oats still left to sow before they become submissive members of society. Undoubtedly, all men are not equally fit subjects for civilization; and because the majority, like dogs and sheep, are tame by inherited disposition, this is no reason why the others should have their natures broken that they may be reduced to the same level. Men are in the main alike, but they were made several in order that they might be various. If a low use is to be served, one man will do nearly or quite as well as another; if a high one, individual excellence is to be regarded. Any man can stop a hole to keep the wind away, but no other man could serve so rare a use as the author of this illustration did. Confucius says, "The skins of the tiger and the leopard, when they are tanned, are as the skins of the dog and the sheep tanned." But it is not the part of a true culture to tame tigers, any more than it is to make sheep ferocious; and tanning their skins for shoes is not the best use to which they can be put.

When looking over a list of men's names in a foreign language, as of military officers, or of authors who have written on a particular subject, I am reminded once more that there is nothing in a name. The name Menschikoff, for instance, has nothing in it to my ears more human than a whisker, and it may belong to a rat. As the names of the Poles and Russians are to us, so are ours to them. It is as if they had been named by the child's rigmarole, *Iery wiery ichery van, tittle-tol-tan*. I see in my mind a herd of wild creatures swarming over the earth, and to each the herdsman has affixed some barbarous sound in his own dialect. The names of men are, of course, as cheap and meaningless as *Bose* and *Tray*, the names of dogs.

Methinks it would be some advantage to philosophy if men were named merely in the gross, as they are known. It would be necessary only to know the genus and perhaps the race or variety, to know the individual. We are not prepared to believe that every private soldier in a Roman army had a name of his own—because we have not supposed that he had a character of his own.

At present our only true names are nicknames. I knew a boy who, from his peculiar energy, was called "Buster" by his playmates, and this rightly supplanted his Christian name. Some travelers tell us that an Indian had no name given him at first, but earned it, and his name was his fame; and among some tribes he acquired a new name with every new exploit. It is pitiful when a man bears a name for convenience merely, who has earned neither name nor fame.

I will not allow mere names to make distinctions for me, but still see men in herds for all them. A familiar name cannot make a man less strange to me. It may be given to a savage who retains in secret his own wild title earned in the woods. We have a wild savage in us, and a savage name is perchance somewhere recorded as ours. I see that my neighbor, who bears the familiar epithet William or Edwin, takes it off with his jacket. It does not adhere to him when asleep or in anger, or aroused by any passion or inspiration. I seem to hear pronounced by some of his kin at such a time his original wild name in some jaw-breaking or else melodious tongue.

Here is this vast, savage, hovering mother of ours, Nature, lying all around, with such beauty, and such affection for her children, as the leopard; and yet we are so early weaned from her breast to society, to that culture which is exclusively an interaction of man on man—a sort of breeding in and in, which produces at most a merely English nobility, a civilization destined to have a speedy limit.

In society, in the best institutions of men, it is easy to detect a certain precocity. When we should still be growing children, we are already little men. Give me a culture which imports much muck from the meadows, and deepens the soil—not that which trusts to heating manures, and improved implements and modes of culture only!

Many a poor sore-eyed student that I have heard of would grow faster, both intellectually and physically, if, instead of sitting up so very late, he honestly slumbered a fool's allowance.

There may be an excess even of informing light. Niepce, a Frenchman, discovered "actinism," that power in the sun's rays which produces a chemical effect; that granite rocks, and stone structures, and statues of metal "are all alike destructively acted upon during the hours of sunshine, and, but for provisions of Nature no less wonderful, would soon perish under the delicate touch of the most subtile of the agencies of the universe." But he observed that "those bodies which underwent this change during the daylight possessed the power of restoring themselves to their original conditions during the hours of night, when this excitement was no longer influencing them." Hence it has been inferred that "the hours of darkness are as necessary to the inorganic creation as we know night and sleep are to the organic kingdom." Not even does the moon shine every night, but gives place to darkness.

I would not have every man nor every part of a man cultivated, any more than I would have every acre of earth cultivated: part will be tillage, but the greater part will be meadow and forest, not only serving an immediate use, but preparing a mould against a distant future, by the annual decay of the vegetation which it supports.

There are other letters for the child to learn than those which Cadmus invented. The Spaniards have a good term to express this wild and dusky knowledge, *Gramatica parda*, tawny grammar, a kind of mother-wit derived from that same leopard to which I have referred.

We have heard of a Society for the Diffusion of Useful Knowledge. It is said that knowledge is power, and the like. Methinks there is equal need of a Society for the Diffusion of Useful Ignorance, what we will call Beautiful Knowledge, a knowledge useful in a higher sense: for what is most of our boasted so-called knowledge but a conceit that we know something, which robs us of the advantage of our actual ignorance? What we call knowledge is often our positive ignorance; ignorance our negative knowledge. By long years of patient industry and reading of the newspapers—for what are the libraries of science but files of newspapers?—a man accumulates a myriad facts, lays them up in his memory, and then when in some spring of his life he saunters abroad into the Great Fields of thought, he, as it were, goes to grass like a horse and leaves all his harness behind in the stable. I would say to the Society for the Diffusion of Useful Knowledge, sometimes, Go to grass. You have eaten hay long enough. The spring has come with its green crop. The very cows are driven to their country pastures before the end of May; though I have heard of one unnatural farmer who kept his cow in the barn and fed her on hay all the year round. So, frequently, the Society for the Diffusion of Useful Knowledge treats its cattle.

A man's ignorance sometimes is not only useful, but beautiful—while his knowledge, so called, is oftentimes worse than useless, besides being ugly. Which is the best man to deal with—he who knows nothing about a subject, and, what is extremely rare, knows that he knows nothing, or he who really knows something about it, but thinks that he knows all?

My desire for knowledge is intermittent, but my desire to bathe my head in atmospheres unknown to my feet is perennial and constant. The highest that we can attain to is not Knowledge, but Sympathy with Intelligence. I do not know that this higher knowledge amounts to anything more definite than a novel and grand surprise on a sudden revelation of the insufficiency of all that we called Knowledge before—a discovery that there are more things in heaven and earth than are dreamed of in our philosophy. It is the lighting up of the mist by the sun. Man cannot *know* in any higher sense than this, any more than he can look serenely and with impunity in the face of the sun: Ὡς τὶ νοῶν, οὐ χεῖνον νοήσεις, "You will not perceive that, as perceiving a particular thing," say the Chaldean Oracles.

There is something servile in the habit of seeking after a law which we may obey. We may study the laws of matter at and for our convenience, but a successful life knows no law. It is an unfortunate discovery certainly, that of a law which binds us where we did not know before that we were bound. Live free, child of the mist—and with respect to knowledge we are all children of the mist. The man who takes the liberty to live is superior to all the laws, by virtue of his relation to the lawmaker. "That is active duty," says the Vishnu Purana, "which is not for our bondage; that is knowledge which is for our liberation: all other duty is good only unto weariness; all other knowledge is only the cleverness of an artist."

It is remarkable how few events or crises there are in our histories, how little exercised we have been in our minds, how few experiences we have had. I would fain be assured that I am growing apace and rankly, though my very growth disturb this dull equanimity—though it be with struggle through long, dark, muggy nights or seasons of gloom. It would be well if all our lives were a divine tragedy even, instead of this trivial comedy or farce. Dante, Bunyan, and others appear to have been exercised in their minds more than we: they were subjected to a kind of culture such as our district schools and colleges do not contemplate. Even Mahomet, though many may scream at his name, had a good deal more to live for, aye, and to die for, than they have commonly.

When, at rare intervals, some thought visits one, as perchance he is walking on a railroad, then, indeed, the cars go by without his hearing them. But soon, by some inexorable law, our life goes by and the cars return.

"Gentle breeze, that wanderest unseen,
And bendest the thistles round Loira of storms,
Traveler of the windy glens,
Why hast thou left my ear so soon?"

While almost all men feel an attraction drawing them to society, few are attracted strongly to Nature. In their reaction to Nature men appear to me for the most part, notwithstanding their arts, lower than the animals. It is not often a beautiful relation, as in the case of the animals. How little appreciation of the beauty of the land-scape there is among us! We have to be told that the Greeks called the world Κόσμος, Beauty, or Order, but we do not see clearly why they did so, and we esteem it at best only a curious philological fact.

For my part, I feel that with regard to Nature I live a sort of border life, on the confines of a world into which I make occasional and transient forays only, and my patriotism and allegiance to the state into whose territories I seem to retreat are those of a moss-trooper. Unto a life which I call natural I would gladly follow even a will-o'-the-wisp through bogs and sloughs unimaginable, but no moon nor firefly has shown me the causeway to it. Nature is a personality so vast and universal that we have never seen one of her features. The walker in the familiar fields which stretch around my native town sometimes finds himself in another land than is described in their owners' deeds, as it were in some faraway field on the confines of the actual Concord, where her jurisdiction ceases, and the idea which the word Concord suggests ceases to be suggested. These farms which I have myself surveyed, these bounds which I have set up, appear dimly still as through a mist; but they have no chemistry to fix them; they fade from the surface of the glass, and the picture which the painter painted stands out dimly from beneath. The world with which we are commonly acquainted leaves no trace, and it will have no anniversary.

I took a walk on Spaulding's Farm the other afternoon. I saw the setting sun lighting up the opposite side of a stately pine wood. Its golden rays straggled into the aisles of the wood as into some noble hall. I was impressed as if some ancient and altogether admirable and shining family had settled there in that part of the land called Concord, unknown to me—to whom the sun was servant—who had not gone into society in the village—who had not been called on. I saw their park, their pleasure-ground, beyond through the wood, in Spaulding's cranberry-meadow. The pines furnished them with gables as they grew. Their house was not obvious to vision; the trees grew through it. I do not know whether I heard the sounds of a suppressed hilarity or not. They seemed to recline on the sunbeams. They have sons and daughters. They are quite well. The farmer's cart-path, which leads directly through their hall, does not in the least put them out, as the muddy bottom of a pool is sometimes seen through the reflected skies. They never heard of Spaulding, and do not know that he is their neighbor—notwithstanding I heard him whistle as he drove his team through the house. Nothing can equal the serenity of their lives. Their coat-of-arms is simply a lichen. I saw it painted on the pines and oaks. Their attics were in the tops of the trees. They are of no politics. There was no noise of labor. I did not perceive that they were weaving or spinning. Yet I did detect, when the wind lulled and hearing was done away, the finest imaginable sweet musical hum, as of a distant hive in May—which perchance was the sound of their thinking. They had no idle thoughts, and no one without could see their work, for their industry was not as in knots and excrescences embayed.

But I find it difficult to remember them. They fade irrevocably out of my mind even now while I speak, and endeavor to recall them and recollect myself. It is only after a long and serious effort to recollect my best thoughts that I become again aware of their cohabitancy. If it were not for such families as this, I think I should move out of Concord.

We are accustomed to say in New England that few and fewer pigeons visit us every year. Our forests furnish no mast for them. So, it would seem, few and fewer thoughts visit each growing man from year to year, for the grove in our minds is laid waste—sold to feed unnecessary fires of ambition, or sent to mill—and there is scarcely a twig left for them to perch on. They no longer build nor breed with us. In some more genial season, perchance, a faint shadow flits across the landscape of the mind, cast by the *wings* of some thought in its vernal or autumnal migration, but, looking up, we are unable to detect the substance of the thought itself. Our winged thoughts are turned to poultry. They no longer soar, and they attain only to a Shanghai and Cochin-China grandeur. Those *gra-a-ate thoughts*, those *gra-a-ate* men you hear of!

We hug the earth—how rarely we mount! Methinks we might elevate ourselves a little more. We might climb a tree, at least. I found my account in climbing a tree once. It was a tall white pine, on the top of a hill; and though I got well pitched, I was well paid for it, for I discovered new mountains in the horizon which I had never seen before—so much more of the earth and the heavens. I might have walked about the foot of the tree for threescore years and ten, and yet I certainly should never have seen them. But, above all, I discovered around me—it was near the end of June—on the ends of the topmost branches only, a few minute and delicate red conelike blossoms, the fertile flower of the white pine looking heavenward. I carried straightway to the village the topmost spire, and showed it to stranger jurymen who walked the streets—for it was court week—and to farmers and lumber-dealers and woodchoppers and hunters, and not one had ever seen the like before, but they wondered as at a star dropped down. Tell of ancient architects finishing their works on the tops of columns as perfectly as on the lower and more visible parts! Nature has from the first expanded the minute blossoms of the forest only toward the heavens, above men's heads and unobserved by them. We see only the flowers that are under our feet in the meadows. The pines have developed their delicate blossoms on the highest twigs of the wood every summer for ages, as well over the heads of Nature's red children as of her white ones; yet scarcely a farmer or hunter in the land has ever seen them.

Above all, we cannot afford not to live in the present. He is blessed over all mortals who loses no moment of the passing life in remembering the past. Unless our philosophy hears the cock crow in every barnyard within our horizon, it is belated. That sound commonly reminds us that we are growing rusty and antique in our employments and habits of thoughts. His philosophy comes down to a more recent time than ours. There is something suggested by it that is a newer testament—the gospel according to this moment. He has not fallen astern; he has got up early and kept up early, and to be where he is is to be in season, in the foremost rank of time. It is an expression of the health and soundness of Nature, a brag for all the world—healthiness as of a spring burst forth, a new fountain of the Muses, to celebrate this last instant of time. Where he lives no fugitive slave laws are passed. Who has not betrayed his master many times since last he heard that note?

The merit of this bird's strain is in its freedom from all plaintiveness. The singer can easily move us to tears or to laughter, but where is he who can excite in us a pure morning joy? When, in doleful dumps, breaking the awful stillness of our wooden sidewalk on a Sunday, or, perchance, a watcher in the house of mourning, I hear a cockerel crow far or near, I think to myself, "There is one of us well, at any rate," and with a sudden gush return to my senses.

We had a remarkable sunset one day last November. I was walking in a meadow, the source of a small brook, when the sun at last, just before setting, after a cold, gray day, reached a clear stratum in the horizon, and the softest, brightest morning sunlight fell on the dry grass and on the stems of the trees in the opposite horizon and on the leaves of the shrub oaks on the hillside, while our shadows stretched long over the meadow eastward, as if we were the only motes in its beams. It was such a light as we could not have imagined a moment before, and the air also was so warm and serene that nothing was wanting to make a paradise of that meadow. When we reflected that this was not a solitary phenomenon, never to happen again, but that it would happen forever and ever, an infinite number of evenings, and cheer and reassure the latest child that walked there, it was more glorious still.

The sun sets on some retired meadow, where no house is visible, with all the glory and splendor that it lavishes on cities, and perchance as it has never set before—where there is but a solitary marsh hawk to have his wings gilded by it, or only a musquash looks out from his cabin, and there is some little black-veined brook in the midst of the marsh, just beginning to meander, winding slowly round a decaying stump. We walked in so pure and bright a light, gilding the withered grass and leaves, so softly and serenely bright, I thought I had never bathed in such a golden flood, without a ripple or a murmur to it. The west side of every wood and rising ground gleamed like the boundary of Elysium, and the sun on our backs seemed like a gentle herdsman driving us home at evening.

So we saunter toward the Holy Land, till one day the sun shall shine more brightly than ever he has done, shall perchance shine into our minds and hearts, and light up our whole lives with a great awakening light, as warm and serene and golden as on a bankside in autumn.

'Rejoicing in wildness'

John Muir

The American Forests
1897

THE forests of America, however slighted by man, must have been a great delight to God; for they were the best he ever planted. The whole continent was a garden, and from the beginning it seemed to be favored above all the other wild parks and gardens of the globe. To prepare the ground, it was rolled and sifted in seas with infinite loving deliberation and fore-thought, lifted into the light, submerged and warmed over and over again, pressed and crumpled into folds and ridges, mountains, and hills, subsoiled with heaving volcanic fires, ploughed and ground and sculptured into scenery and soil with glaciers and rivers,—every feature growing and changing from beauty to beauty, higher and higher. And in the fullness of time it was planted in groves, and belts, and broad, exuberant, mantling forests, with the largest, most varied, most fruitful, and most beautiful trees in the world. Bright seas made its border, with wave embroidery and icebergs; gray deserts were outspread in the middle of it, mossy tundras on the north, savannas on the south, and blooming prairies and plains; while lakes and rivers shone through all the vast forests and openings, and happy birds and beasts gave delightful animation. Everywhere, everywhere over all the blessed continent, there were beauty, and melody, and kindly, wholesome, foodful abundance.

These forests were composed of about five hundred species of trees, all of them in some way useful to man, ranging in size from twenty-five feet in height and less than one foot in diameter at the ground to four hundred feet in height and more than twenty feet in diameter,—lordly monarchs proclaiming the gospel of beauty like apostles. For many a century after the ice-ploughs were melted, nature fed them and dressed them every day; working like a man, a loving, devoted, painstaking gardener; fingering every leaf and flower and mossy furrowed bole; bending, trimming, modeling, balancing, painting them with the loveliest colors; bringing over them now clouds with cooling shadows and showers, now sunshine; fanning them with gentle winds and rustling their leaves; exercising them in every fibre with storms, and pruning them; loading them with flowers and fruit, loading them with snow, and ever making them more beautiful as the years rolled by. Wide-branching oak and elm in endless variety, walnut and maple, chestnut and beech, ilex and locust, touching limb to limb, spread a leafy translucent canopy along the coast of the Atlantic over the wrinkled folds and ridges of the Alleghanies,—a green billowy sea in summer, golden and purple in autumn, pearly gray like a steadfast frozen mist of interlacing branches and sprays in leafless, restful winter.

To the southward stretched dark, level-topped cypresses in knobby, tangled swamps, grassy savannas in the midst of them like lakes of light, groves of gay, sparkling spice-trees, magnolias and palms, glossy-leaved and blooming and shining continually. To the northward, over Maine and Ottawa, rose hosts of spiry, rosiny evergreens,—white pine and spruce, hemlock and cedar, shoulder to shoulder, laden with purple cones, their myriad needles sparkling and shimmering, covering hills and swamps, rocky headlands and domes, ever bravely aspiring and seeking the sky; the ground in their shade now snow-clad and frozen, now mossy and flowery; beaver meadows here and there, full of lilies and grass; lakes gleaming like eyes, and a silvery embroidery of rivers and creeks watering and brightening all the vast glad wilderness.

Thence westward were oak and elm, hickory and tupelo, gum and liriodendron, sassafras and ash, linden and laurel, spreading on ever wider in glorious exuberance over the great fertile tile basin of the Mississippi, over damp level bottoms, low dimpling hollows, and round dotting hills, embosoming sunny prairies and cheery park openings, half sunshine, half shade; while a dark wilderness of pines covered the region around the Great Lakes. Thence still westward swept the forests to right and left around grassy plains and deserts a thousand miles wide: irrepressible hosts of spruce and pine, aspen and willow, nut-pine and juniper, cactus and yucca, caring nothing for drought, extending undaunted from mountain to mountain, over mesa and desert, to join the darkening multitudes of pines that covered the high Rocky ranges and the glorious forests along the coast of the moist and balmy Pacific, where new species of pine, giant cedars and spruces, silver firs and sequoias, kings of their race, growing close together like grass in a meadow, poised their brave domes and spires in the sky three hundred feet above the ferns and the lilies that enameled the ground; towering serene through the long centuries, preaching God's forestry fresh from heaven.

Here the forests reached their highest development. Hence they went wavering northward over icy Alaska, brave spruce and fir, poplar and birch, by the coasts and the rivers, to within sight of the Arctic Ocean. American forests! the glory of the world! Surveyed thus from the east to the west, from the north to the south, they are rich beyond thought, immortal, immeasurable, enough and to spare for every feeding, sheltering beast and bird, insect and son of Adam; and nobody need have cared had there been no pines in Norway, no cedars and deodars on Lebanon and the Himalayas, no vine-clad selvas in the basin of the Amazon. With such variety, harmony, and triumphant exuberance, even nature, it would seem, might have rested content with the forests of North America, and planted no more.

So they appeared a few centuries ago when they were rejoicing in wildness. The Indians with stone axes could do them no more harm than could gnawing beavers and browsing moose. Even the fires of the Indians and the fierce shattering lightning seemed to work together only for good in clearing spots here and there for smooth garden prairies, and openings for sunflowers seeking the light. But when the steel axe of the white man rang out in the startled air their doom was sealed. Every tree heard the bodeful sound, and pillars of smoke gave the sign in the sky.

I suppose we need not go mourning the buffaloes. In the nature of things they had to give place to better cattle, though the change might have been made without barbarous wickedness. Likewise many of nature's five hundred kinds of wild trees had to make way for orchards and cornfields. In the settlement and civilization of the country, bread more than timber or beauty was wanted; and in the blindness of hunger, the early settlers, claiming Heaven as their guide, regarded God's trees as only a larger kind of pernicious weeds, extremely hard to get rid of. Accordingly, with no eye to the future, these pious destroyers waged interminable forest wars; chips flew thick and fast; trees in their beauty fell crashing by millions, smashed to confusion, and the smoke of their burning has been rising to heaven more than two hundred years. After the Atlantic coast from Maine to Georgia had been mostly cleared and scorched into melancholy ruins, the overflowing multitude of bread and money seekers poured over the Alleghanies into the fertile middle West, spreading ruthless devastation ever wider and farther over the rich valley of the Mississippi and the vast shadowy pine region about the Great Lakes. Thence still westward the invading horde of destroyers called settlers made its fiery way over the broad Rocky Mountains, felling and burning more fiercely than ever, until at last it has reached the wild side of the continent, and entered the last of the great aboriginal forests on the shores of the Pacific.

Surely, then, it should not be wondered at that lovers of their country, bewailing its baldness, are now crying aloud, "Save what is left of the forests!" Clearing has surely now gone far enough; soon timber will be scarce, and not a grove will be left to rest in or pray in. The remnant protected will yield plenty of timber, a perennial harvest for every right use, without further diminution of its area, and will continue to cover the springs of the rivers that rise in the mountains and give irrigating waters to the dry valleys at their feet, prevent wasting floods and be a blessing to everybody forever.

Every other civilized nation in the world has been compelled to care for its forests, and so must we if waste and destruction are not to go on to the bitter end, leaving America as barren as Palestine or Spain. In its calmer moments in the midst of bewildering hunger and war and restless over-industry, Prussia has learned that the forest plays an important part in human progress, and that the advance in civilization only makes it more indispensable. It has, therefore, as shown by Mr. Pinchot, refused to deliver its forests to more or less speedy destruction by permitting them to pass into private ownership. But the state woodlands are not allowed to lie idle. On the contrary, they are made to produce as much timber as is possible without spoiling them. In the administration of its forests, the state righteously considers itself bound to treat them as a trust for the nation as a whole, and to keep in view the common good of the people for all time.

In France no government forests have been sold since 1870. On the other hand, about one half of the fifty million francs spent on forestry has been given to engineering works, to make the replanting of denuded areas possible. The disappearance of the forests in the first place, it is claimed, may be traced in most cases directly to mountain pasturage. The provisions of the code concerning private woodlands are substantially these: No private owner may clear his woodlands without giving notice to the government at least four months in advance, and the forest service may forbid the clearing on the following grounds: to maintain the soil on mountains, to defend the soil against erosion and flooding by rivers or torrents, to insure the existence of springs or watercourses, to protect the dunes and seashore, etc. A proprietor who has cleared his forest without permission is subject to heavy fine, and in addition may be made to replant the cleared area.

In Switzerland, after many laws like our own had been found wanting, the Swiss forest school was established in 1865, and soon after the Federal Forest Law was enacted, which is binding over nearly two thirds of the country. Under its provisions, the cantons must appoint and pay the number of suitably educated foresters required for the fulfillment of the forest law; and in the organization of a normally stocked forest, the object of first importance must be the cutting each year of an amount of timber equal to the total annual increase, and no more.

The Russian government passed a law in 1888, declaring that clearing is forbidden in protected forests, and is allowed in others "only when its effects will not be to disturb the suitable relations which should exist between forest and agricultural lands."

Even Japan is ahead of us in the management of her forests. They cover an area of about 29,000,000 acres. The feudal lords valued the woodlands, and enacted vigorous protective laws; and when, in the latest civil war, the Mikado government destroyed the feudal system, it declared the forests that had belonged to the feudal lords to be the property of the state, promulgated a forest law binding on the whole kingdom, and founded a school of forestry in Tokio. The forest service does not rest satisfied with the present proportion of woodland, but looks to planting the best forest trees it can find in any country, if likely to be useful and to thrive in Japan.

In India systematic forest management was begun about forty years ago, under difficulties—presented by the character of the country, the prevalence of running fires, opposition from lumbermen, settlers, etc.—not unlike those which confront us now. Of the total area of government forests, perhaps 70,000,000 acres, 55,000,000 acres have been brought under the control of the forestry department,—a larger area than that of all our national parks and reservations. The chief aims of the administration are effective protection of the forests from fire, an efficient system of regeneration, and cheap transportation of the forest products; the results so far have been most beneficial and encouraging.

It seems, therefore, that almost every civilized nation can give us a lesson on the management and care of forests. So far our government has done nothing effective with its forests, though the best in the world, but is like a rich and foolish spendthrift who has inherited a magnificent estate in perfect order, and then has left his fields and meadows, forests and parks, to be sold and plundered and wasted at will, depending on their inexhaustible abundance. Now it is plain that the forests are not inexhaustible, and that quick measures must be taken if ruin is to be avoided. Year by year the remnant is growing smaller before the axe and fire, while the laws in existence provide neither for the protection of the timber from destruction nor for its use where it is most needed.

As is shown by Mr. E. A. Bowers, formerly Inspector of the Public Land Service, the foundation of our protective policy, which has never protected, is an act passed March 1, 1817, which authorized the Secretary of the Navy to reserve lands producing live-oak and cedar, for the sole purpose of supplying timber for the navy of the United States. An extension of this law by the passage of the act of March 2, 1831, provided that if any person should cut live-oak or red cedar trees or other timber from the lands of the United States for any other purpose than the construction of the navy, such person should pay a fine nor less than triple the value of the timber cut, and be imprisoned for a period not exceeding twelve months. Upon this old law, as Mr. Bowers points out, having the construction of a wooden navy in view, the United States government has to-day chiefly to rely in protecting its timber throughout the arid regions of the West, where none of the naval timber which the law had in mind is to be found.

By the act of June 3, 1878, timber can be taken from public lands not subject to entry under any existing laws except for minerals, by *bona fide* residents of the Rocky Mountain States and Territories and the Dakotas. Under the timber and stone act, of the same date, land in the Pacific States and Nevada, valuable mainly for timber, and unfit for cultivation if the timber is removed, can be purchased for two dollars and a half an acre, under certain restrictions. By the act of March 3, 1875, all land-grant and right-of-way railroads are authorized to take timber from the public lands adjacent to their lines for construction purposes; and they have taken it with a vengeance, destroying a hundred times more than they have used, mostly by allowing fires to run in the woods. The settlement laws, under which a settler may enter lands valuable for timber as well as for agriculture, furnish another means of obtaining title to public timber.

With the exception of the timber culture act, under which, in consideration of planting a few acres of seedlings, settlers on the treeless plains got 160 acres each, the above is the only legislation aiming to protect and promote the planting of forests. In no other way than under some one of these laws can a citizen of the United States make any use of the public forests. To show the results of the timber-planting act, it need only be stated that of the 38,000,000 acres entered under it, less than 1,000,000 acres have been patented. This means that less than 50,000 acres have been planted with stunted, woebegone, almost hopeless sprouts of trees, while at the same time the government has allowed millions of acres of the grandest forest trees to be stolen, or destroyed, or sold for nothing. Under the act of June 3, 1878, settlers in Colorado and the Territories were allowed to cut timber for mining and educational purposes from mineral land, which in the practical West means both cutting and burning anywhere and everywhere, for any purpose, on any sort of public land. Thus, the prospector, the miner, and mining and railroad companies are allowed by law to take all the timber they like for their mines and roads, and the forbidden settler, if there are no mineral lands near his farm or stock-ranch, or none that he knows of, can hardly be expected to forbear taking what he needs wherever he can find it. Timber is as necessary as bread, and no scheme of management failing to recognize and properly provide for this want can possibly be maintained. In any case, it will be hard to teach the pioneers that it is wrong to steal government timber. Taking from the government is with them the same as taking from nature, and their consciences flinch no more in cutting timber from the wild forests than in drawing water from a lake or river. As for reservation and protection of forests, it seems as silly and needless to them as protection and reservation of the ocean would be, both appearing to be boundless and inexhaustible.

The special land agents employed by the General Land Office to protect the public domain from timber depredations are supposed to collect testimony to sustain prosecution, and to superintend such prosecution on behalf of the government, which is represented by the district attorneys. But timber-thieves of the Western class are seldom convicted, for the good reason that most of the jurors who try such cases are themselves as guilty as those on trial. The effect of the present confused, discriminating, and unjust system has been to place almost the whole population in opposition to the government; and as conclusive of its futility, as shown by Mr. Bowers, we need only state that during the seven years from 1881 to 1887 inclusive the value of the timber reported stolen from the government lands was $36,719,935, and the amount recovered was $478,073, while the cost of the services of special agents alone was $455,000, to which must be added the expense of the trials. Thus for nearly thirty-seven million dollars' worth of timber the government got less than nothing; and the value of that consumed by running fires during the same period, without benefit even to thieves, was probably over two hundred millions of dollars. Land commissioners and Secretaries of the Interior have repeatedly called attention to this ruinous state of affairs, and asked Congress to enact the requisite legislation for reasonable reform. But, busied with tariffs, etc., Congress has given no heed to these or other appeals, and our forests, the most valuable and the most destructible of all the natural resources of the country, are being robbed and burned more rapidly than ever. The annual appropriation for so-called "protection service" is hardly sufficient to keep twenty-five timber agents in the field, and as far as any efficient protection of timber is concerned these agents themselves night as well be timber.

That a change from robbery and ruin to a permanent rational policy is urgently needed nobody with the slightest knowledge of American forests will deny. In the East and along the northern Pacific coast, where the rainfall is abundant, comparatively few care keenly what becomes of the trees as long as fuel and lumber are not noticeably dear. But in the Rocky Mountains and California and Arizona, where the forests are inflammable, and where the fertility of the lowlands depends upon irrigation, public opinion is growing stronger every year in favor of permanent protection by the federal government of all the forests that cover the sources of the streams. Even lumbermen in these regions, long accustomed to steal, are now willing and anxious to buy lumber for their mills under cover of law: some possibly from a late second growth of honesty, but most, especially the small mill-owners, simply because it no longer pays to steal where all may not only steal, but also destroy, and in particular because it costs about as much to steal timber for one mill as for ten, and therefore the ordinary lumberman can no longer compete with the large corporations. Many of the miners find that timber is already becoming scarce and dear on the denuded hills around their mills, and they too are asking for protection of forests, at least against fire. The slow-going, un-thrifty farmers, also, are beginning to realize that when the timber is stripped from the mountains the irrigating streams dry up in summer, and are destructive in winter; that soil, scenery, and everything slips off with the trees: so of course they are coming into the ranks of tree-friends.

Of all the magnificent coniferous forests around the Great Lakes, once the property of the United States, scarcely any belong to it now. They have disappeared in lumber and smoke, mostly smoke, and the government got not one cent for them; only the land they were growing on was considered valuable, and two and a half dollars an acre was charged for it. Here and there in the Southern States there are still considerable areas of timbered government land, but these are comparatively unimportant. Only the forests of the West are significant in size and value, and these, although still great, are rapidly vanishing. Last summer, of the unrivaled redwood forests of the Pacific Coast Range, the United States Forestry Commission could not find a single quarter-section that remained in the hands of the government.

Under the timber and stone act of 1878, which might well have been called the "dust and ashes act," any citizen of the United States could take up one hundred and sixty acres of timber land, and by paying two dollars and a half an acre for it obtain title. There was some virtuous effort made with a view to limit the operations of the act by requiring that the purchaser should make affidavit that he was entering the land exclusively for his own use, and by not allowing any association to enter more than one hundred and sixty acres. Nevertheless, under this act wealthy corporations have fraudulently obtained title to from ten thousand to twenty thousand acres or more. The plan was usually as follows: A mill company desirous of getting title to a large body of redwood or sugar-pine land first blurred the eyes and ears of the land agents, and then hired men to enter the land they wanted, and immediately deed it to the company after a nominal compliance with the law; false swearing in the wilderness against the government being held of no account. In one case which came under the observation of Mr. Bowers, it was the practice of a lumber company to hire the entire crew of every vessel which might happen to touch at any port in the redwood belt, to enter one hundred and sixty acres each and immediately deed the land to the company, in consideration of the company's paying all expenses and giving the jolly sailors fifty dollars apiece for their trouble.

By such methods have our magnificent redwoods and much of the sugar-pine forests of the Sierra Nevada been absorbed by foreign and resident capitalists. Uncle Sam is not often called a fool in business matters, yet he has sold millions of acres of timber land at two dollars and a half an acre on which a single tree was worth more than a hundred dollars. But this priceless land has been patented, and nothing can be done now about the crazy bargain. According to the everlasting law of righteousness, even the fraudulent buyers at less than one per cent of its value are making little or nothing, on account of fierce competition. The trees are felled, and about half of each giant is left on the ground to be converted into smoke and ashes; the better half is sawed into choice lumber and sold to citizens of the United States or to foreigners: thus robbing the country of its glory and impoverishing it without right benefit to anybody,—a bad, black business from beginning to end.

The redwood is one of the few conifers that sprout from the stump and roots, and it declares itself willing to begin immediately to repair the damage of the lumberman and also that of the forest-burner. As soon as a redwood is cut down or burned it sends up a crowd of eager, hopeful shoots, which, if allowed to grow, would in a few decades attain a height of a hundred feet, and the strongest of them would finally become giants as great as the original tree. Gigantic second and third growth trees are found in the redwoods, forming magnificent temple-like circles around charred ruins more than a thousand years old. But not one denuded acre in a hundred is allowed to raise a new forest growth. On the contrary, all the brains, religion, and superstition of the neighborhood are brought into play to prevent a new growth. The sprouts from the roots and stumps are cut off again and again, with zealous concern as to the best time and method of making death sure. In the clearings of one of the largest mills on the coast we found thirty men at work, last summer, cutting off redwood shoots "in the dark of the moon," claiming that all the stumps and roots cleared at this auspicious time would send up no more shoots. Anyhow, these vigorous, almost immortal trees are killed at last, and black stumps are now their only monuments over most of the chopped and burned areas.

The redwood is the glory of the Coast Range. It extends along the western slope, in a nearly continuous belt about ten miles wide, from beyond the Oregon boundary to the south of Santa Cruz, a distance of nearly four hundred miles, and in massive, sustained grandeur and closeness of growth surpasses all the other timber woods of the world. Trees from ten to fifteen feet in diameter and three hundred feet high are not uncommon, and a few attain a height of three hundred and fifty feet, or even four hundred, with a diameter at the base of fifteen to twenty feet or more, while the ground beneath them is a garden of fresh, exuberant ferns, lilies, gaultheria, and rhododendron. This grand tree, *Sequoia sempervirens*, is surpassed in size only by its near relative, *Sequoia gigantea*, or big tree, of the Sierra Nevada, if indeed it is surpassed. The sempervirens is certainly the taller of the two. The gigantea attains a greater girth, and is heavier, more noble in port, and more sublimely beautiful. These two sequoias are all that are known to exist in the world, though in former geological times the genus was common and had many species. The redwood is restricted to the Coast Range, and the big tree to the Sierra.

As timber the redwood is too good to live. The largest sawmills ever built are busy along its seaward border, "with all the modern improvements," but so immense is the yield per acre it will be long ere the supply is exhausted. The big tree is also to some extent being made into lumber. Though far less abundant than the redwood, it is, fortunately, less accessible, extending along the western flank of the Sierra in a partially interrupted belt about two hundred and fifty miles long, at a height of from four to eight thousand feet above the sea. The enormous logs, too heavy to handle, are blasted into manageable dimensions with gunpowder. A large portion of the best timber is thus shattered and destroyed, and, with the huge knotty tops, is left in ruins for tremendous fires that kill every tree within their range, great and small. Still, the species is not in danger of extinction. It has been planted and is flourishing over a great part of Europe, and magnificent sections of the aboriginal forests have been reserved as national and state parks,—the Mariposa Sequoia Grove, near Yosemite, managed by the State of California, and the General Grant and Sequoia national parks on the King's, the Kaweah, and Tule rivers, efficiently guarded by a small troop of United States cavalry under the direction of the Secretary of the Interior. But there is not a single specimen of the redwood in any national park. Only by gift or purchase, so far as I know, can the government get back into its possession a single acre of this wonderful forest.

The legitimate demands on the forests that have passed into private ownership, as well as those in the hands of the government, are increasing every year with the rapid settlement and upbuilding of the country, but the methods of lumbering are as yet grossly wasteful. In most mills only the best portions of the best trees are used, while the ruins are left on the ground to feed great fires which kill much of what is left of the less desirable timber, together with the seedlings on which the permanence of the forest depends. Thus every mill is a centre of destruction far more severe from waste and fire than from use. The same thing is true of the mines, which consume and destroy indirectly immense quantities of timber with their innumerable fires, accidental or set to make open ways, and often without regard to how far they run. The prospector deliberately sets fires to clear off the woods just where they are densest, to lay the rocks bare and make the discovery of mines easier. Sheep-owners and their shepherds also set fires everywhere through the woods in the fall to facilitate the march of their countless flocks the next summer, and perhaps in some places to improve the pasturage. The axe is not yet at the root of every tree, but the sheep is, or was before the national parks were established and guarded by the military, the only effective and reliable arm of the government free from the blight of politics. Not only do the shepherds, at the driest time of the year, set fire to everything that will burn, but the sheep consume every green leaf, not sparing even the young conifers when they are in a starving condition from crowding, and they rake and dibble the loose soil of the mountain sides for the spring floods to wash away, and thus at last leave the ground barren.

Of all the destroyers that infest the woods the shake-maker seems the happiest. Twenty or thirty years ago, shakes, a kind of long boardlike shingles split with a mallet and a frow, were in great demand for covering barns and sheds, and many are used still in preference to common shingles, especially those made from the sugar-pine, which do not warp or crack in the hottest sunshine. Drifting adventurers in California, after harvest and threshing are over, oftentimes meet to discuss their plans for the winter, and their talk is interesting. Once, in a company of this kind, I heard a man say, as he peacefully smoked his pipe: "Boys, as soon as this job's done I'm goin' into the duck business. There's big money in it, and your grub costs nothing. Tule Joe made five hundred dollars last winter on mallard and teal. Shot 'em on the Joaquin, tied 'em in dozens by the neck, and shipped 'em to San Francisco. And when he was tired wading in the sloughs and touched with rheumatiz, he just knocked off on ducks, and went to the Contra Costa hills for dove and quail. It's a mighty good business, and you're your own boss, and the whole thing's fun."

Another of the company, a bushy-bearded fellow, with a trace of brag in his voice, drawled out: "Bird business is well enough for some, but bear is my game, with a deer and a California lion thrown in now and then for change. There's always market for bear grease, and sometimes you can sell the hams. They're good as hog hams any day. And you are your own boss in my business, too, if the bears ain't too big and too many for you. Old grizzlies I despise,—they want cannon to kill 'em; but the blacks and browns are beauties for grease, and when once I get 'em just right, and draw a bead on 'em, I fetch 'em every time." Another said he was going to catch up a lot of mustangs as soon as the rains set in, hitch them to a gang-plough, and go to farming on the San Joaquin plains for wheat. But most preferred the shake business, until something more profitable and as sure could be found, with equal comfort and independence.

With a cheap mustang or mule to carry a pair of blankets, a sack of flour, a few pounds of coffee, and an axe, a frow, and a cross-cut saw, the shake-maker ascends the mountains to the pine belt where it is most accessible, usually by some mine or mill road. Then he strikes off into the virgin woods, where the sugar-pine, king of all the hundred species of pines in the world in size and beauty, towers on the open sunny slopes of the Sierra in the fullness of its glory. Selecting a favorable spot for a cabin near a meadow with a stream, he unpacks his animal and stakes it out on the meadow. Then he chops into one after another of the pines, until he finds one that he feels sure will split freely, cuts this down, saws off a section four feet long, splits it, and from this first cut, perhaps seven feet in diameter, he gets shakes enough for a cabin and its furniture,—walls, roof, door, bedstead, table, and stool. Besides his labor, only a few pounds of nails are required. Sapling poles form the frame of the airy building, usually about six feet by eight in size, on which the shakes are nailed, with the edges overlapping. A few bolts from the same section that the shakes were made from are split into square sticks and built up to form a chimney, the inside and interspaces being plastered and filled in with mud. Thus, with abundance of fuel, shelter and comfort by his own fireside are secured. Then he goes to work sawing and splitting for the market, tying the shakes in bundles of fifty or a hundred. They are four feet long, four inches wide, and about one fourth of an inch thick. The first few thousands he sells or trades at the nearest mill or store, getting provisions in exchange. Then he advertise, in whatever way he can, that he has excellent sugar-pine shakes for sale, easy of access and cheap.

Only the lower, perfectly clear, free-splitting portions of the giant pines are used,—perhaps ten to twenty feet from a tree two hundred and fifty in height; all the rest is left a mass of ruins, to rot or to feed the forest fires, while thousands are hacked deeply and rejected in proving the grain. Over nearly all of the more accessible slopes of the Sierra and Cascade mountains in southern Oregon, at a height of from three to six thousand feet above the sea, and for a distance of about six hundred miles, this waste and confusion extends. Happy robbers! dwelling in the most beautiful woods, in the most salubrious climate, breathing delightful odors both day and night, drinking cool living water,—roses and lilies at their feet in the spring, shedding fragrance and ringing bells as if cheering them on in their desolating work. There is none to say them nay. They buy no land, pay no taxes, dwell in a paradise with no forbidding angel either from Washington or from heaven. Every one of the frail shake shanties is a centre of destruction, and the extent of the ravages wrought in this quiet way is in the aggregate enormous.

It is not generally known that, notwithstanding the immense quantities of timber cut every year for foreign and home markets and mines, from five to ten times as much is destroyed as is used, chiefly by running forest fires that only the federal government can stop. Travelers through the West in summer are not likely to forget the fire-work displayed along the various railway tracks. Thoreau, when contemplating the destruction of the forests on the east side of the continent, said that soon the country would be so bald that every man would have to grow whiskers to hide its nakedness, but he thanked God that at least the sky was safe. Had he gone West he would have found out that the sky was not safe; for all through the summer months, over most of the mountain regions, the smoke of mill and forest fires is so thick and black that no sunbeam can pierce it. The whole sky, with clouds, sun, moon, and stars, is simply blotted out. There is no real sky and no scenery. Not a mountain is left in the landscape. At least none is in sight from the lowlands, and they all might as well be on the moon, as far as scenery is concerned.

The half dozen transcontinental railroad companies advertise the beauties of their lines in gorgeous many-colored folders, each claiming its as the "scenic route." "The route of superior desolation" —the smoke, dust, and ashes route— would be a more truthful description. Every train rolls on through dismal smoke and barbarous melancholy ruins; and the companies might well cry in their advertisements: "Come! travel our way. Ours is the blackest. It is the only genuine Erebus route. The sky is black and the ground is black, and on either side there is a continuous border of black stumps and logs and blasted trees appealing to heaven for help as if still half alive, and their mute eloquence is most interestingly touching. The blackness is perfect. On account of the superior skill of our workmen, advantages of climate, and the kind of trees, the charring is generally deeper along our line, and the ashes are deeper, and the confusion and desolation displayed can never be rivaled. No other route on this continent so fully illustrates the abomination of desolation." Such a claim would be reasonable, as each seems the worst, whatever route you chance to take.

Of course a way had to be cleared through the woods. But the felled timber is not worked up into firewood for the engines and into lumber for the company's use; it is left lying in vulgar confusion, and is fired from time to time by sparks from locomotives or by the workmen camping along the line. The fires, whether accidental or set, are allowed to run into the woods as far as they may, thus assuring comprehensive destruction. The directors of a line that guarded against fires, and cleared a clean gap edged with living trees, and fringed and mantled with the grass and flowers and beautiful seedling that are ever ready and willing to spring up, might justly boast of the beauty of their road; for nature is always ready to heal every scar. But there is no such road on the western side of the continent. Last summer, in the Rocky Mountains, I saw six fires started by sparks from a locomotive within a distance of three miles, and nobody was in sight to prevent them from spreading. They might run into the adjacent forests and burn the timber from hundreds of square miles; not a man in the State would care to spend an hour in fighting them, as long as his own fences and buildings were not threatened.

Notwithstanding all the waste and use which have been going on unchecked like a storm for more than two centuries, it is not yet too late, though it is high time, for the government to begin a rational administration of its forests. About seventy million acres it still owns,—enough for all the country, if wisely used. These residual forests are generally on mountain slopes, just where they are doing the most good, and where their removal would be followed by the greatest number of evils; the lands they cover are too rocky and high for agriculture, and can never be made as valuable for any other crop as for the present crop of trees. It has been shown over and over again that if these mountains were to be stripped of their trees and underbrush, and kept bare and sodless by hordes of sheep and the innumerable fires the shepherds set, besides those of the millmen, prospectors shake-makers, and all sorts of adventurers, both lowlands and mountains would speedily become little better than deserts, compared with their present beneficent fertility. During heavy rainfalls and while the winter accumulations of snow were melting, the larger streams would swell into destructive torrents, cutting deep, rugged-edged gullies, carrying away the fertile humus and soil as well as sand and rocks, filling up and overflowing their lower channels, and covering the lowland fields with raw detritus. Drought and barrenness would follow.

In their natural condition, or under wise management, keeping out destructive sheep, preventing fires, selecting the trees that should be cut for lumber, and preserving the young ones and the shrubs and sod of herbaceous vegetation, these forests would be a never failing fountain of wealth and beauty. The cool shades of the forest give rise to moist beds and currents of air, and the sod of grasses and the various flowering plants and shrubs thus fostered, together with the network and sponge of tree roots, absorb and hold back the rain and the waters from melting snow, compelling them to ooze and percolate and flow gently through the soil in streams that never dry. All the pine needles and rootlets and blades of grass, and the fallen decaying trunks of trees, are dams, storing the bounty of the clouds and dispensing it in perennial life-giving streams, instead of allowing it to gather suddenly and rush headlong in short-lived devastating floods. Everybody on the dry side of the continent is beginning to find this out, and, in view of the waste going on, is growing more and more anxious for government protection. The outcries we hear against forest reservations come mostly from thieves who are wealthy and steal timber by wholesale. They have so long been allowed to steal and destroy in peace that any impediment to forest robbery is denounced as a cruel and irreligious interference with "vested rights," likely to endanger the repose of all ungodly welfare.

> Gold, gold, gold! How strong a voice that metal has!
> "O wae for the siller, it is saepreva'lin'."

Even in Congress, a sizable chunk of gold, carefully concealed, will outtalk and outfight all the nation on a subject like forestry, well smothered in ignorance, and in which the money interests of only a few are conspicuously involved. Under these circumstances, the bawling, blethering oratorical stuff drowns the voice of God himself. Yet the dawn of a new day in forestry is breaking. Honest citizens see that only the rights of the government are being trampled, not those of the settlers. Merely what belongs to all alike is reserved, and every acre that is left should be held together under the federal government as a basis for a general policy of administration for the public good. The people will not always be deceived by selfish opposition, whether from lumber and mining corporations or from sheepmen and prospectors, however cunningly brought forward underneath fables and gold.

Emerson says that things refuse to be mismanaged long. An exception would seem to be found in the case of our forests, which have been mismanaged rather long, and now come desperately near being like smashed eggs and spilt milk. Still, in the long run the world does not move backward. The wonderful advance made in the last few years, in creating four national parks in the West, and thirty forest reservations, embracing nearly forty million acres; and in the planting of the borders of streets and highways and spacious parks in all the great cities, to satisfy the natural taste and hunger for landscape beauty and righteousness that God has put, in some measure, into every human being and animal, shows the trend of awakening public opinion. The making of the far-famed New York Central Park was opposed by even good men, with misguided pluck, perseverance, and ingenuity; but straight right won its way, and now that park is appreciated. So we confidently believe it will be with our great national parks and forest reservations. There will be a period of indifference on the part of the rich, sleepy with wealth, and of the toiling millions, sleepy with poverty, most of whom never saw a forest; a period of screaming protest and objection from the plunderers, who are as unconscionable and enterprising as Satan. But light is surely coming, and the friends of destruction will preach and bewail in vain.

The United States government has always been proud of the welcome it has extended to good men of every nation, seeking freedom and homes and bread. Let them be welcomed still as nature welcomes them, to the woods as well as to the prairies and plains. No place is too good for good men, and still there is room. They are invited to heaven, and may well be allowed in America. Every place is made better by them. Let them be as free to pick gold and gems from the hills, to cut and hew, dig and plant, for homes and bread, as the birds are to pick berries from the wild bushes, and moss and leaves for nests. The ground will be glad to feed them, and the pines will come down from the mountains for their homes as willingly as the cedars came from Lebanon for Solomon's temple. Nor will the woods be the worse for this use, or their benign influences be diminished any more than the sun is diminished by shining. Mere destroyers, however, tree-killers, spreading death and confusion in the fairest groves and gardens ever planted, let the government hasten to cast them out and make an end of them. For it must be told again and again, and be burningly borne in mind, that just now, while protective measures are being deliberated languidly, destruction and use are speeding on faster and farther every day. The axe and saw are insanely busy, chips are flying thick as snowflakes, and every summer thousands of acres of priceless forests, with their underbrush, soil, springs, climate, scenery, and religion, are vanishing away in clouds of smoke, while, except in the national parks, not one forest guard is employed.

All sorts of local laws and regulations have been tried and found wanting, and the costly lessons of our own experience, as well as that of every civilized nation, show conclusively that the fate of the remnant of our forests is in the hands of the federal government, and that if the remnant is to be saved at all, it must be saved quickly.

Any fool can destroy trees. They cannot run away; and if they could, they would still be destroyed,—chased and hunted down as long as fun or a dollar could be got out of their bark hides, branching horns, or magnificent bole backbones. Few that fell trees plant them; nor would planting avail much towards getting back anything like the noble primeval forests. During a man's life only saplings can be grown, in the place of the old trees—tens of centuries old— that have been destroyed. It took more than three thousand years to make some of the trees in these Western woods,— trees that are still standing in perfect strength and beauty, waving and singing in the mighty forests of the Sierra. Through all the wonderful, eventful centuries since Christ's time—and long before that—God has cared for these trees, saved them from drought, disease, avalanches, and a thousand straining, leveling tempests and floods; but he cannot save them from fools,—only Uncle Sam can do that.

'An Immortal Emerson Night'

Editor's Note: In 1871, John Muir met Ralph Waldo Emerson for the first and only time. In "The Forests of the Yosemite Park," Muir recounted their meeting.

BUT the noble oaks and all these rock-shading, stream-embowering trees are as nothing amid the vast abounding billowy forests of conifers. During my first years in the Sierra I was ever calling on everybody within reach to admire them, but I found no one half warm enough until Emerson came. I had read his essays, and felt sure that of all men he would best interpret the sayings of these noble mountains and trees. Nor was my faith weakened when I met him in Yosemite. He seemed as serene as a sequoia, his head in the empyrean; and forgetting his age, plans, duties, ties of every sort, I proposed an immeasurable camping trip back in the heart of the mountains. He seemed anxious to go, but considerately mentioned his party. I said: "Never mind. The mountains are calling; run away, and let plans and parties and dragging lowland duties all gang tapsal-teerie. We'll go up a cañon singing your own song, 'Good-by, proud world! I'm going home,' in divine earnest. Up there lies a new heaven and a new earth; let us go to the show." But alas, it was too late, too near the sundown of his life. The shadows were growing long, and he leaned on his friends. His party, full of indoor philosophy, failed to see the natural beauty and fullness of promise of my wild plan, and laughed at it in good-natured ignorance, as if it were necessarily amusing to imagine that Boston people might be led to accept Sierra manifestations of God at the price of rough camping. Anyhow, they would have none of it, and held Mr. Emerson to the hotels and trails.

After spending only five tourist days in Yosemite he was led away, but I saw him two days more; for I was kindly invited to go with the party as far as the Mariposa big trees. I told Mr. Emerson that I would gladly go to the sequoias with him, if he would camp in the grove. He consented heartily, and I felt sure that we would have at least one good wild memorable night around a sequoia camp-fire. Next day we rode through the magnificent forests of the Merced basin, and I kept calling his attention to the sugar pines, quoting his wood-notes, "Come listen what the pine tree saith," etc., pointing out the noblest as kings and high priests, the most eloquent and commanding preachers of all the mountain forests, stretching forth their century-old arms in benediction over the worshiping congregations crowded about them. He gazed in devout admiration, saying but little, while his fine smile faded away.

Early in the afternoon, when we reached Clark's Station, I was surprised to see the party dismount. And when I asked if we were not going up into the grove to camp they said: "No; it would never do to lie out in the night air. Mr. Emerson might take cold; and you know, Mr. Muir, that would be a dreadful thing." In vain I urged, that only in homes and hotels were colds caught, that nobody ever was known to take cold camping in these woods, that there was not a single cough or sneeze in all the Sierra. Then I pictured the big climate-changing, inspiring fire I would make, praised the beauty and fragrance of sequoia flame, told how the great trees would stand about us transfigured in the purple light, while the stars looked down between the great domes; ending by urging them to come on and make an immortal

Emerson night of it. But the house habit was not to be overcome, nor the strange dread of pure night air, though it is only cooled day air with a little dew in it. So the carpet dust and unknowable reeks were preferred. And to think of this being a Boston choice! Sad commentary on culture and the glorious transcendentalism.

Accustomed to reach whatever place I started for, I was going up the mountain alone to camp, and wait the coming of the party next day. But since Emerson was so soon to vanish, I concluded to stop with him. He hardly spoke a word all the evening, yet it was a great pleasure simply to be near him, warming in the light of his face as at a fire. In the morning we rode up the trail through a noble forest of pine and fir into the famous Mariposa Grove, and stayed an hour or two, mostly in ordinary tourist fashion, looking at the biggest giants, measuring them with a tape line, riding through prostrate fire-bored trunks, etc., though Mr. Emerson was alone occasionally, sauntering about as if under a spell. As we walked through a fine group, he quoted, "There were giants in those days," recognizing the antiquity of the race. To commemorate his visit, Mr. Galen Clark, the guardian of the grove, selected the finest of the unnamed trees and requested him to give it a name. He named it Samoset, after the New England sachem, as the best that occurred to him.

The poor bit of measured time was soon spent, and while the saddles were being adjusted I again urged Emerson to stay. "You are yourself a sequoia," I said. "Stop and get acquainted with your big brethren." But he was past his prime, and was now as a child in the hands of his affectionate but sadly civilized friends, who seemed as full of old-fashioned conformity as of bold intellectual independence. It was the afternoon of the day and the afternoon of his life, and his course was now westward down all the mountains into the sunset. The party mounted and rode away in wondrous contentment, apparently, tracing the trail through ceanothus and dogwood bushes, around the bases of the big trees, up the slope of the sequoia basin, and over the divide. I followed to the edge of the grove. Emerson lingered in the rear of the train, and when he reached the top of the ridge, after all the rest of the party were over and out of sight, he turned his horse, took off his hat and waved me a last good-by. I felt lonely, so sure had I been that Emerson of all men would be the quickest to see the mountains and sing them. Gazing awhile on the spot where he vanished, I sauntered back into the heart of the grove, made a bed of sequoia plumes and ferns by the side of a stream, gathered a store of firewood, and then walked about until sundown. The birds, robins, thrushes, warblers, etc., that had kept out of sight, came about me, now that all was quiet, and made cheer. After sundown I built a great fire, and as usual had it all to myself. And though lonesome for the first time in these forests, I quickly took heart again,—the trees had not gone to Boston, nor the birds; and as I sat by the fire, Emerson was still with me in spirit, though I never again saw him in the flesh. He sent books and wrote, cheering me on; advised me not to stay too long in solitude. Soon he hoped that my guardian angel would intimate that my probation was at a close. Then I was to roll up my herbariums, sketches, and poems (though I never knew I had any poems), and come to his house; and when I tired of him and his humble surroundings, he would show me to better people.

But there remained many a forest to wander through, many a mountain and glacier to cross, before I was to see his Wachusett and Monadnock, Boston and Concord. It was seventeen years after our parting on the Wawona ridge that I stood beside his grave under a pine tree on the hill above Sleepy Hollow. He had gone to higher Sierras, and, as I fancied, was again waving his hand in friendly recognition.

THE WALDEN WOODS PROJECT

www.walden.org   781.259.4700

A NONPROFIT organization, the Walden Woods Project is committed to preserving the land, literature, and legacy of Henry David Thoreau through conservation, education, research, and advocacy. Founded by recording artist Don Henley, the Project uses the land it has protected in Walden Woods to foster an ethic of environmental stewardship and social responsibility, both cornerstones of Thoreau's philosophy. The Project opens its library to all those wishing to advance their understanding of the literature and legacy of Henry David Thoreau. Among the materials the Thoreau Institute at Walden Woods acquired in November 2014 were two manuscript leaves from Thoreau's "Walking" essay, one of which is reproduced here (at right) for the first time in a book.

YOSEMITE CONSERVANCY

www.yosemiteconservancy.org   800.469.7275

THROUGH the support of donors, Yosemite Conservancy provides grants and support to Yosemite National Park to help preserve and protect Yosemite today and for future generations. The work funded by Yosemite Conservancy is visible throughout the park, from trail rehabilitation to wildlife protection and habitat restoration. The Conservancy is dedicated to enhancing the visitor experience and providing a deeper connection to the park through outdoor programs, volunteering and wilderness services. Yosemite Conservancy supporters carry forward John Muir's passion for Yosemite.

Manuscript leaf from Thoreau's "Walking"

About Scot Miller

SCOT Miller is an award-winning photographer whose work has formed the basis of numerous books, including *Walden: The 150th Anniversary Illustrated Edition of the American Classic; Cape Cod: Illustrated Edition of the American Classic; First Light: Five Photographers Explore Yosemite's Wilderness; My First Summer in the Sierra: 100th Anniversary Illustrated Edition,* winner of a 2011 National Outdoor Book Award; and *Thoreau, The Maine Woods: A Photographic Journey Through an American Wilderness.* He is a frequent contributor to the "Moment in Nature" videos, broadcast nationally on the Emmy Award-winning *CBS Sunday Morning* show. His photographic and video collaborations include work with Yosemite Conservancy, the Walden Woods Project, and the Harvard Museum of Natural History. *Emerson, Muir, Thoreau: A Photographic Trilogy of American Wildness* is Scot's sixth book.

Scot's photographs have been featured in exhibitions at the Harvard Museum of Natural History; the Peabody Museum of Archaeology and Ethnology at Harvard University; the Thoreau Institute at Walden Woods; the Crystal Bridges Museum of American Art in Bentonville, Arkansas; the Ansel Adams Gallery in Yosemite National Park; the Dallas Museum of Natural History; the Franklin Institute in Philadelphia; Turtle Bay Exploration Park in Redding, California; the North Carolina Forestry Museum; the Cincinnati Museum Center; and other venues across the country. Scot lives in Dallas, Texas, with his wife, Marilyn, where they own and operate the Sun to Moon Gallery, a fine-art photography gallery.

For more on Scot and the photographs in this book, visit www.ScotMiller.com.

The Photographs in the Artist's View

MANY years ago, at a time when I was searching for artistic direction with my photography, a wise man told me to just follow my muse. I took that to mean, above all else: do what you enjoy, what you believe in, what you're passionate about. It was advice well taken. Following my heart, the years have found me on interesting paths, many of which are reflected in this book.

Photographically, this book is about experiences, journeys, and places I visited over a seventeen-year period. It is also about playing a supporting role in commemorating the inspired writings of Emerson, Muir, and Thoreau, and presenting them in a new and most deserved light.

The photographs were created from October 1997 to October 2014, each conveying the spirit of a particular moment (some longer than others), a feeling, or a sense of place. Sixty-six photographs were captured with medium-format film cameras (6x7cm and 6x17cm), the remaining three with digital cameras. Seventy percent were created in national or state parks/forests.

The sequencing of images, with accompanying quotations, was driven by the photographs (light, color, form, shape), so the text narrative unfolds from page to page in a somewhat random manner. There is, however, a common thread throughout the book—a rewarding relationship with, and passion for, nature, with an eye toward conservation and preservation. Interspersing select quotations from each man's essay and pairing them with photographic images combine to present a fresh body of work, one that honors the prescience of the authors and, I hope, inspires readers to celebrate America's legacy of wild and open spaces.

ACKNOWLEDGMENTS

THIS is a special book for me, incorporating a wider range of imagery, both geographic and subject-wise, than any of my previous books. It gives me great pleasure to pay homage to three icons of the early American conservation movement. Thank you to Levenger Press for making it possible. A special thank-you goes out to editor Mim Harrison, along with designer Danielle Furci and color technician Alfred Guerra, for their hard work and dedication to making this the best edition possible.

Nonprofit organizations like Yosemite Conservancy and the Walden Woods Project are crucial to protecting and preserving our country's wild and open spaces, and I am pleased to highlight the good work they and similar organizations throughout the country are doing to carry the legacy forward.

Four of the photographs were taken at the LBJ Ranch, part of the Lyndon B. Johnson National Historical Park, where I am artist-in-park. Thank you to Superintendent Russ Whitlock for his support and friendship, and to the welcoming park staff for embracing my artistry and making me feel at home.

It was President Johnson who signed the Wilderness Act of 1964 into law, creating the legal definition for wilderness in the United States and protecting millions of acres of federal land. I am thankful to have had the opportunity to spend much quality time in wilderness areas, following my muse and practicing the art of photography.

The extent of my wilderness photography would not have been possible without the friendship and camaraderie of a talented group of photographer friends: Charles Cramer, Karl Kroeber, Mike Osborne, and Keith Walklet. Over the last fifteen years, I have had the pleasure of spending time with them on extended trips into the Yosemite and Sierra Nevada wilderness. Ten photographs from these backcountry adventures are presented in these pages.

My photography trips often require extended stays away from home, many times totally out of touch, and it is especially comforting to have the love, support, and encouragement of an understanding partner. Thank you, Marilyn Fox Miller. This book is dedicated to you.

Index of Images by State

Ozark National Scenic Riverways, Missouri   October 31, 2008

Uncommon Books for Thoughtful Readers

Levenger Press is the publishing arm of

L E V E N G E R ®

Levengerpress.com   800.544.0880

To write your review of this book or any Levenger Press title,
please visit Levenger.com and type the book title into the Search box.

"What I began by reading, I must finish by acting."
Henry David Thoreau